LAUNCHING A NEW WORSHIP COMMUNITY

A Practical Guide for the 2020s

Paul Nixon

and

Craig Gilbert

DISCIPLESHIP
RESOURCES
NASHVILLE

CONTENTS

ACKNOWLEDGMENTS

From Paul

My life as a ministry coach is a meandering river of conversation with frontline church leaders. An idea raised by a British client at 6:00 a.m. will inspire an afternoon conversation with someone in California. Without these amazing people—hundreds of them across the past two decades—I could not begin to see the big picture of the trends and paradigm shifts that are underway globally. So I want to thank all my clients, who are my eyes and ears in a variety of cultural contexts!

From Craig

To my wife, Catherine, who has supported and encouraged me from the beginning, I owe everything. Her intelligence, common sense and abiding love make me better than I could ever be on my own. Thank you to my daughter, Elizabeth, whose penetrating insight, love of others and deep love of God inspires me in my daily walk. Thank you to my son,

Austin, for the many years of working beside me as my partner in ministry as he developed his own path to serving God.

Thank you to my parents, Kenneth and Carolyn, for laying a solid foundation of faith on which I could build and for always being there to pray me through every situation. To my sister, Candice, who I know keeps me in prayer. I also owe an eternal debt of gratitude to my grandparents, J. D. and Dotty, whose example I strive to follow every day.

I am grateful to all the churches, pastors, leaders, and musicians with whom I have served. Thank you to the leaders of the Texas Annual Conference for allowing me to share my efforts in worship design and renewal. I am also grateful to the faculty of the Robert E. Webber Institute for Worship Studies for guiding me to this incredible world of worship.

Finally, thank you to my coauthor, Paul Nixon. He believed in me enough to invite me to work with him in ministry. I will be forever grateful for that support.

ORIENTATION

Paul Nixon

Once upon a time, in another millennium, I served a church with three worship services back-to-back on Sunday morning. These services were roughly identical, except for the uneven quality of music from one to the next.[1] The least developed of the three was the 9:30 a.m. service. We became convinced that if this service could be reimagined and then reintroduced to our community, we could fill the house to overflowing at this time of the morning. We studied the worship innovators of that time. We took surveys, both of our church's worshipers and the larger public. It was clear that to be effective, significant changes would be required: a change of musical leadership, the abandonment of clergy vestments, the addition of a drama troupe, fresh strategies for crafting hospitality and community, and a rethinking of how we invite people to express commitment. Clarity emerged around the vision and content for the new service, but the challenge of putting it all together felt overwhelming—building the teams, getting the word out, and finding people to fill the room.

Thankfully, I ran across a book by Charles Arn titled *How to Start a New Worship Service*.[2] Arn offered a concise agenda of things to do to get ready to launch a new worship service in 1990s America. Using that book, we created an action timeline for a new 9:30 a.m. service.

We worked our plan. We launched. We continued to experiment with new elements and then backed off, only to try them again, creating a sense of experimentation and innovation that gave energy and expectancy to this worship community.

The room began to fill, pushing folks into the balcony. More people came to faith. Worship attendance jumped. And in the years that followed, with the same basic road map, our church launched additional new services, expanding to three locations and reaching more than 1,000 people each Sunday.

As my work shifted to consulting and coaching early in this century, **my lead suggestion for church renewal was for churches to launch new worship gatherings, designed as boldly as possible, with (and for) new people.** This led to four consecutive years of net growth for our denominational region after two decades of collective numerical decline.[3] Most of our long-existing worship communities continued their gentle, steady aging and shrinking; but by adding new communities (usually under the umbrella of existing congregations), we were able to counter the losses and find net gains collectively.

Many of those new worship communities planted twenty years ago have now themselves plateaued or fallen into decline. Even churches that were thriving as late as the first quarter of 2020 (before the COVID-19 pandemic) are now scrambling. A new ministry moment greets us, with radically changing sensibilities and life habits, in almost every zip code.

In an age when organized religion is often associated with backward thinking, a large share of the population in the English-speaking world has given up on the church. It is beyond their imagination that church could offer anything good and relevant for them. Thus, more front-end work is now required to build community relationships and cultivate trust before people will engage with us. In today's world, new and innovative worship communities are needed more than ever; yet the work can be tough.

The COVID-19 pandemic pushed churches all over the world to get their worship experiences online. A burst of global trial and error ensued. The initial results were mixed, but many churches soon reported experiencing significant increases in weekly engagements[4] of thirty minutes or more, as compared to pre-pandemic participation. However, the newness of digital worship wore off eventually. Engagement dissipated somewhat as the months of the pandemic wore on and as screen fatigue set in. Furthermore, the impact of a large digital gathering is far different from gathering in an actual room full of people and energy. The potential distractions from a digital worship experience in one's living room seem infinite. Yet the convenience and the positive experiences of millions of people open up possibilities for digital worship that also seem unlimited.

As we move deeper into this decade, many live/in-person worship gatherings will be accompanied by a digital gathering. Following a 1990s road map will clearly not be adequate to help us effectively plant a new worship community in the years ahead.

Each year, the organizations that I am a part of help scores of churches launch new worship communities.[5] This work is constantly morphing. The variety of worship styles and venues has exploded. The typical size of the gatherings today is smaller than we would have seen with the same amount of work twenty years ago. Two decades ago, in the United States, we often worked to get more than 125 people ready to launch a new worship community, knowing that the people dynamics of a large launch would be such that the community would be able to grow far beyond 125 members. This is still possible in some places. **But in many communities, if we waited for 125 people before launching, we would simply never launch at all.** Hence, we now focus on how to launch smaller-venue communities that can take root, grow, and multiply over time. And if we launch online first and then move to offering a physical gathering, there is almost no minimum critical mass (or minimum number of worshipers) required to start.

Best practices in church planting are radically shifting. With the social disruptions of 2020 and 2021, it is almost as if we are now awakening to the year 2030. So fast did the rate of social change speed up, it feels like we were flung ten years into our future. Even young people may be feeling a Rumpelstiltskin-like grade of disorientation.

Hence, this book!

You may be planting a church, in which you will soon launch a first worship community. Or you may be seeking to renew a church by launching a fresh worship community alongside more-established worship services. Or you may be thinking further outside of the box in terms of a new model for church. In any case, you will need a clear vision—and, with it, a fresh road map—to weave all the critical tasks into a plan.

This book should help you devise your road map for launching a new worship community, given the challenges of the 2020s and beyond. It is organized into thirty-two succinct chapters, written by sixteen different people. In some places, you may detect a certain echo or redundancy of ideas between the chapters. If you stumble across the same big idea stated three different ways by three different authors, please take note! That repeated idea will most likely be something requiring your serious consideration. Only a few persons on your launch team will need to read every chapter; in many cases, a leader/reader might simply focus on those particular chapters most relevant to their part of a project.[6] In the table of contents, Craig Gilbert and I have indicated the chapters that we feel are of maximal relevance for all team members by placing them in **bold** type.

Nearly two-thirds of the chapters were written by Craig Gilbert and by me, with the remainder contributed by members and friends of the Epicenter Group, each of whom was invited into this project because of their particular ministry genius. You will encounter a range of perspectives throughout these chapters. Not everything you read may fit into your team's conversation. Use what you can, and toss what you can't. **I suggest grabbing a stack of sticky notes or a highlighter so that, as you read through this book, you can flag any page that discusses a topic or idea you would like to work into the timeline of ministry development for your new worship community.** In a few words, write on the sticky note the type of idea or action involved. When you are finished reading, you can use the sticky notes to begin creating your action timeline on a fresh sheet of paper, noting references to the appropriate pages in this book. Hopefully, you will discover helpful insights pooled together in a way that will enable you and your team to articulate the nature of your task for your context and build a plan that will lead to a happy ministry launch.

We wish you the best in this endeavor, and we offer you an invitation. If you convene a launch team that looks like the new worship community you desire to plant, we invite your team to read this book together and join us for regularly scheduled cohorts of launch teams, within the framework of a new initiative called Launch Parties. As a part of these Launch Parties, we will offer four hours of teaching for your team, followed by four coaching sessions. We hope that scores of churches will bring teams to one of the Launch Parties, as we get serious about relaunching ministry in the post-pandemic years.

Then, *after your launch*, the **Epicenter Group** would like to unpack what happened with your ministry. With the unpacking session, you would agree to share some raw video footage from your launch event(s). You would grant us rights to use the recordings in creating a training video for others. The Epicenter Group cannot guarantee this for every church that asks, but we encourage you to ask! To explore this opportunity, please reach out to me, Paul Nixon, at paul@epicentergroup.org.

WELCOME

Craig Gilbert

I want to say to you, "Welcome!"

Welcome is a word that goes beyond a mere hello. *Welcome* says not only do I acknowledge that we are together but also I am *happy* about it! It says that I want to share this space with you. I want you to settle in and get comfy. Then, it says let's spend some quality time together.

I have been following God's call on my life to lead others in worship for a long time. Early in my life, God called me to begin new worship services. Sometimes this meant starting a new service from scratch. Sometimes it meant ending a service first and then rebuilding it to fit a new need for worship in that church. In every instance, being involved in designing and building a new worship service meant that I had a front-row seat to see what God can do when leaders say "Yes!" to God's will.

I am going to assume that you are hearing that same voice, urging you to branch into new territories, following God's will through worship at your church. You are going to get to see our amazing God go to work right beside you and in front of you. If your experience ends up being anything like mine, God will also be coming along behind you, picking up broken pieces and cleaning up messes.

For my part in writing this book, a good bit of it is about us—you and me—doing this together. My guess is you probably haven't ever thought of the authors as being with you on the journey through a book like this and in the process that follows. I know that when I read a book on this topic, I always assume I am following a path the author has already walked. The book then becomes a guide, so that I can benefit from it as I follow a similar path.

This book gave me the opportunity to share my experiences. But in writing these stories, I walked along the path again myself. The difference for me was that I was writing with you in mind. Each time I wrote a chapter, I walked a familiar path but tried to see it through your eyes, in a post-COVID world. I wanted to be able to describe this amazing opportunity as an experienced builder would and yet to connect to the enthusiasm, excitement, and—yes—even fear someone has in starting a new worship service for the first time.

So why do I begin with "Welcome"? Because that is precisely what a new worship service should accomplish. With this new worship community, you will be welcoming people who are walking into worship for the first time, walking in for the first time in a long time, and walking in out of a long-standing habit. If we want to be truly welcoming and in a real relationship with these people who are answering our invitation—and God's—to worship together, then we must be experienced worshipers who still know how to connect to all of the emotions a new person feels. It can't just be the "same old, same old" for us; no, it has to be "new every morning" (Lam. 3:23).

And that is why I say, "Welcome!" We are standing at the beginning of this path together. I have walked it before, and I am certain I will walk it again. This time, I am going to walk it with you. Are you ready?

Then, let's go! I can't wait to see where God will lead us.

God, open our hearts to the words ahead. May they pierce our comfortable façade and provoke in us deep praying and listening as we begin this new ministry journey. Amen.

1

LEADING IN THIS MINISTRY MOMENT

Beth Ann Estock

We're window-shopping.

We pretend it's something you hunt the world for,
or it's sold only in the most exclusive markets.

Friend, unlike a pearl, it's already in your hand.
It is within you.
Let go of everything else
and there it is.
What won't you trade for it?
Ah, there you are.

Listen: unlike a pearl
you can't have or hold it:
it's a realm, a whole people.
It's for the world, not you.
That may be the hardest thing to let go of.
When you do—
there it is.

—STEVE GARNAAS-HOLMES

COVID-19 invited us to see beyond our communities, to consider this big, blue "dot," spinning in the Milky Way. People in every country experienced the pandemic together, facing uncertainty and fear. In its wake, multiple crises remained. We had to ponder the long-term loss of institutions and jobs. Some of us are still wondering how we are going to feed and educate our families in a new economy. Many of us are awakening to and caring about, as if for the first time, the effects of racial injustice in our healthcare and criminal justice systems. We are growing more aware of how interconnected with and dependent upon the health of our planet we are, as we face the effects of climate change. It seems that when we are forced to suspend our normal life patterns, new perspectives and possibilities arise before us.

We are beginning to see fissures and cracks in long-standing institutions, revealing their brittleness and the corrupted values that are trying to hold them together. People with power in the old decaying orders hold onto their control at the expense of the common good—at the expense of kingdom values of doing justice, embodying loving-kindness, and walking humbly with God.

In business, in government, and in the church, we have fallen down the rabbit hole and found ourselves in the valley of the shadow of death, asking, *What do I need to let go of that is no longer working? What are my fears that keep me stuck? What is the truth that I am running away from?*

We, as church leaders, have come to a threshold place and moment. The Spirit is calling for something new that will manifest itself only when we have the courage to step across the threshold, into the unknown. Where is the Spirit calling us to go? Love demands that we lead in new ways. The capacities that we once relied upon as leaders will not be enough to guide us in this liminal time between what was and what is to come.

This concept can be found in the Indo-European root of the word *leader*: *leit.* It means "to die or to step forth." In other words, to lead is to move from one world that we know into another one that we don't know.

A gifted leader is constantly letting go of what was so that she can whole-heartedly step into the unfolding future. This brings us to the root word of *courage*, which is *cor*, the Latin word for *heart*. It means "to speak one's mind by telling all one's heart." A leader listens to the wisdom of his heart as a source of guidance, allowing him to step into the unknown with creativity and grace. This is exactly the kind of leader the church needs today.

What Was

Before the pandemic, the world of church planting typically focused on growing worshiping communities to financial sustainability—a monetized business model, at heart. The end focus was to get ourselves into a building so that we could worship together on Sundays. We used one-to-one conversations, built a lead team, and planted small groups as ways to get to this result. Our basic assumption was that our communities longed for what we were offering; that people were looking for a good church; and that it was up to us, as leaders, to brand and market our way into our neighbors' hearts. The stakes were high, not only for the institution but also for the individual leaders tasked with this mission.

Ministry start-up leaders worked hard to get traction in order to make something happen. As long as they did [*fill in the blank*], then they could be assured of success. And if they weren't successful to the point of [*fill in your metric of success*], then they were often looked upon as lacking in crucial leadership skills. As a result, many gifted leaders ended up feeling like they had been tossed onto the trash heap of failed church starts, marked with the scarlet letter *F* for "Failed Leader" to haunt them for years. And this sense of failure moved up the food chain, reflecting poorly on supervisors and conference leaders. Wishful thinkers at the top of the hierarchy craved stories of success—bragging rights, if you will—that showed their leadership prowess. They were looking for what would keep the church alive; God forbid that the church should die on their watch! This manifested in leadership turf battles, siloed churches, doctrinal infighting, and unnecessary competition. It was a defensive posture of hunkering down in fear and operating out of survival instincts, much like those early apostles behind closed doors in the upper room after Jesus' ascension.

Fear of failure closes hearts and shuts down brain capacity. When we let fear have its way, we are not able to open up to and listen for the realm of grace unfolding all around us. Fear ultimately keeps church leaders in the safe zone, following the patterns of those who came before them. This leads to trying harder and to doing things that no longer work. To be a "good leader," it is implied, is to power through failure, meet your metrics, and follow the formula: *Bend reality to the formula, if you must!*

I get tired just thinking about it. I wonder what we actually have been trying to accomplish with this model. Don't get me wrong—I believe that the goodness, truth, and beauty of the Christian life and witness are needed now more than ever! With declining numbers of Christian worshipers, the United States is losing one of the key ways in which compassion is taught and modeled. Without a prophetic vision and a clear sense of purpose, people perish as they wallow in an existential crisis of meaninglessness. The meaninglessness manifests in any number of ways, from white grievance movements to drug use to homicides. The problem right now is that the church, as it is currently configured, is wallowing in that same crisis of meaninglessness. The only thing we can see is the lingering shadow of what we were, and we long to go back to it. Resurrection people have lost a sense of what we stand for, as we expend our energy standing against our worst fears.

Meanwhile, corporate and government leaders are beginning to wonder whether working for their stock investors and meeting their quarterly metrics at the expense of humanity are worth it: Do we save lives, or do we make money? Do we offer health insurance, or do we feed our stockholders with another tax cut?

Of course, it is rarely *either/or*. Our world longs for leaders who can practice *both/and* thinking and listening. As these leaders experience the symptoms of the violation of life on so many levels, they are beginning to realize that the repair requires a spiritual dimension. It is ironic that as the church clings to the modern era of metrics and survival at all costs, some corporations are slowing, moving into an integrative spiritual awakening.

What Could Be

I yearn for the prophetic witness of the church in its willingness to die and be reborn. Do we actually have faith in the Resurrection? Do we have the capacity to welcome the Pentecost Spirit into our hearts?

Those early apostles in the upper room hunkered down in fear, trying to figure their way out of their predicament. They drew straws (so to speak), probably had some meetings, and advocated for their particular strategies. Meanwhile, the angels were shaking their heads, saying, "They still don't get it, do they?" Then, in blew the Holy Spirit, God's life-giving breath, unhindered by the closed shutters and with a love so fierce that it opened their hearts to tenderness and compassion. It was so transformative that fear did not have power over them anymore.

This is the transformation that is called for today, a stepping into the unknown, trusting in a divine tenderness that can hold us, even in our fear. God calls us to journey from our heads into our hearts, listening for that deeper wisdom that can guide us through all the valleys of death.

Here are some questions to ask ourselves as we pick up the mantle of spiritual leadership for the 2020s; these are questions to ponder first in solitude and then within the community of sisters and brothers who share leadership at church:

- What really matters to me/us?
- How is life calling me/us to serve?

- How does this sense of calling fit with my/our understanding of God?
- For what does my/our heart break?
- What is the calling from the future that I/we feel in my/our heart right now?
- Where am I/where are we glimpsing grace in the form of goodness, truth, or beauty in my/our context?
- How can I/we partner with that energy?
- How can I/we empower people and teams to rise to meet today's challenges with the very best of who we are?

Can you sense the shift? What would your church look like if your ministry aligned with the yearnings of your heart? These kinds of questions can help give us the freedom to step into our full power and call. It helps us to embody a different quality of devotion, commitment, and learning.

Our core work, like that of Jesus, is to be healers and to cultivate communities of healing. Jesus invited his disciples to go into Samaria to discover the realm of grace with people they didn't even know. He instructed them to look for "people of peace"—persons who were open to receiving them and who, in many cases, might serve to connect them to the larger community. Jesus told his disciples to join such people at their tables, to eat what they ate, and to listen deeply to their stories (see Matthew 10:11; Luke 10:6).

Basically, theirs was a ministry of hanging out and doing life together. Then, Jesus said, "When you encounter brokenness, be a healing balm. And before you leave, say something like this: 'Hey, we just saw a glimpse of the realm of God together! Did you see it? Did you feel that love? Did you experience that grace? Wow! Thank you for helping me to see it too.'"

Our own healing and the healing of our world are intertwined. As we step into the world's pain and shine a light on the shadows, those around us become less emotionally numb and disembodied. We discover, yet again, that collective healing can occur as we courageously tend to our own wounds and receive our own healing.

Elaine Health offers a simple contemplative stance that, if we practiced it, would literally transform the world (emphasis added)[1]:

1. **Show up** to God, ourselves, our neighbors, and our world.
2. **Pay attention** to what is there, what is going on inside and outside ourselves.
3. **Cooperate with God** as God invites, instructs, corrects, or encourages in the situation at hand.
4. **Release the outcome** of cooperation with God. Consciously let go of the outcome, recognizing that God is God and we are not.

Our role as leaders in this ministry moment is to look for folks who resonate with our deepest sense of purpose and partner with them; to become, along with them, cocreators of a future of which we currently know not; to discover community with them; to pray with them; to listen and watch for signs of God's presence and movement with them. In some cases, it is the deep sense of purpose in our neighbors marching in the streets that might reawaken our true call to ministry.

Wherever and whenever spiritual community emerges, worship is a normal and expected response, and it doesn't have to be forced. That is why, in this book, we talk about worship *community* and not simply worship *services*. I have a hunch that when we can open our hearts, experience spiritual community, and let go of the outcome, we will discover that the new thing that is formed is better than we ever could have imagined or innovated on our own.

As you pray about the possibility of gathering a fresh spiritual community, I urge you to slow down and pay attention to what the Spirit is up to—within you, within your colleagues, and within your neighbors. God is not calling you to some trendy twist on a tired 1990s thing; instead,

God says, "I am about to do a new thing; now it springs forth, do you not perceive it?" (Isa. 43:19).

2

WHY START A
NEW GATHERING?

Paul Nixon

I f the singular purpose of a church were to address the fellowship concerns of the active members, there would be little point in any of what
we are here to explore. Creating a new gathering, a new circle of community, at a new hour and possibly in a different space—separate and
distinct from the existing worship communities—makes more work for a
lot of people. It ruins any chance that everybody in the church can know
everybody else. In most cases these days—especially after that crazy thing
we call the year 2020—we may be running low on people at our current
service(s). It might seem silly to think about adding another service when
we can't even fill the one(s) we have.

Even if the new gathering is held in the same building immediately
before or after the current service, and even if it costs almost nothing in
additional utilities, it still will cost the church more money—for new
equipment, probably for additional leadership, and sometimes for better
refreshments. If the new gathering will be bringing additional children
into the building, that means additional noise in the hallways and the
need for expanded custodial services. More children could cost still *more*
money for a children's ministry director. Furthermore, the new people

who gather as a new worship community are typically less likely to volunteer to serve on the church's "classic" committees and less likely to help prop up the old ways of being church.

If we are a new (or newly growing) church in the neighborhood, we will likely find that existing churches in that area will have mixed feelings about us, especially if they think we are going to get the people who would otherwise come to *their* church. Ministry colleagues may say, "There are so many churches and worship services in this community already! Why would you start another one?" And, as Beth reminded us in the previous chapter, many projects fail to take root these days. Starting a new gathering could mean a lot of work without, in some cases, a lot of new people!

So, why would we do this? **Let's name some possible reasons:**

- We care about our neighbors enough to design an experience where they can come to the Table meaningfully and comfortably and not just touch the edges of our church's life. The work of launching a new worship community is always about loving our neighbors enough to share the treasure of Christian faith with them.
- If we are a new faith community, we probably intend to launch a weekly public gathering for worship as a part of our ministry design, reaching people who are not likely to attend worship at any of the current, existing churches.
- If we are an existing church, our current worship gatherings are designed around the needs and cultural context of a certain (probably dwindling) population of people. If we want to attract new people or more people, it would be best if we explored with them a different kind of gathering, one that feels more relevant to their life and their world.
- Our church's long-standing worship gathering finally ran out of steam and out of people and ceased to meet. This gave us an opportunity to restart with a new group of people.

- We need a gathering more oriented to a public unfamiliar with in-house stories and traditions.
- We want to gather with a degree of playfulness, informality, and/or interaction that would be disruptive in our existing worship gatherings.
- Increasing numbers of individuals and families in our community are unable to attend our current services due to their work schedules or their children's sports schedules.
- We have grown some leaders (preachers, musicians) whom we wish to deploy, whose own demographics and life experiences enable them to widen our church's age range or cultural diversity. Rather than losing our current staff, we could create a new venue where new leaders can lead.
- The world of only three TV networks, three flavors of ice cream, and three seasonal sports no longer exists and, in fact, is long gone. We now live in a much more fractured world, where there is a diminishing sense of a mainstream culture. Offering clear and distinct niche options is in order for any restaurant, media content provider, or church that wishes to thrive in this century.
- Some of the people whom we reach in ministry would prefer to worship in a different language (or mix of languages) than we use in our current gathering(s).
- We wish to gather in a smaller, more intimate setting than our current worship room offers. (This may be off-campus from where the church typically meets.)
- We are expanding ministry to a second or third ministry location.
- The traffic is getting worse and prohibiting people in parts of our parish area from easily getting into or out of their neighborhoods during the times when we gather.
- Our church's physical space has grown too crowded. (This still happens in quite a few places.) The worship room, the children's

area, the parking lot, and/or the hallways are filled to reasonable capacity, thus limiting our ability to collect any new people. Just because there seems to be enough space in one of these areas does not mean that we have capacity to grow. For example, an over-crowded parking situation can bottleneck a church's growth, even when there seems to be ample space indoors.[1]

- Without an influx of new people, the church will close.[2]

Perhaps several of the above reasons apply to a church's decision to launch a new gathering. In any case, we need to be clear about the reasons we are doing this. Craig Gilbert has competed in Ironman Triathlons. As Craig trained, he recalls his coach telling him that he must have a clear and compelling reason for doing so. This is because no matter how much one trains, no matter how fit one may be, there will come a point in a race of that distance when one hits a "wall." And when that happens, it is the competitor's resolve and nothing more that will get them past that point.

It will be far from obvious to everyone in the church that we need to add another worship gathering—especially if the gatherings we have now are not full. Church people can always find plenty of reasons not to add a new service; so, we had better make our case clearly.

But there is much more to our question of why start a new worship gathering than the reasons we've mentioned for current church members to bless the idea. In today's world, we also must make a case to the public. I call this the *public value proposition*. This proposition tells me why I (as a member of the public) should pay any attention to a new product, business, or ministry. It articulates the value-add for my life, hopefully in relatable cultural language.

Many of our neighbors have lived all or much of their lives without having participated in a church. Most people have driven past our churches on Sunday mornings for years and have assumed that they are not missing out on anything special. So, why would the neighbors want to accept our invitation to come try a new worship gathering? What are we seeking to say to our neighbors with this new ministry? There are many possibilities, several of which could be true for our church. Among them may be the following:

- We offer a more casual and interactive worship experience than most churches.
- We are kid-friendly, and you can choose whether to keep your child with you in the main room or send them to the children's worship programming.
- We enable people who speak Spanish and English to worship together in one room.
- We lead with love and grace: All are fully welcomed and included, regardless of their questions about faith, their sexual orientation, and so on. And we will teach your children a positive Christian faith without promoting social intolerance of their neighbors.
- We are multiethnic: The group you will see gathered for worship is likely to look like what you typically see at your office, your school, or at the nearby big box store.
- The world beats us up six days a week, and none of us needs a seventh day of that; we are all about healing and building people up to live lives that honor God and bless others.
- We use a DJ rather than a live band, which—for some—makes us feel less performance-oriented and gives us greater range in terms of the music we can offer in our worship experience.
- We worship around tables and eat at the same time—and the food is as fresh and excellent as the music![3]
- We offer an experience of ancient traditions from across many centuries in a fresh, contemporary setting.
- We believe life should be beautiful. When we gather, we apply the Christian faith in relevant ways that enable you and your family to be your best selves and live beautiful lives.

- We don't believe in "boring church." Doubtful? Give us a shot, and you will see.
- We offer the kind of music that a lot of people like and would love to see in a church experience.[4]

In every case, we want to create an experience that causes the people we invite into it to respond with, "Wow, I did not know church could be like *that!*"

So What?

In the last couple of pages, we have covered reasons that could explain why some new worship services take root alongside existing ministries, either within our own church or down the street. Ultimately, however, we need a clear sense of why we do church at all; why bother our neighbors with any of this?

Several years ago, I was in the middle of a presentation, challenging a group in a major American city to plant new faith communities. I said to them that if we failed to do so, someone would soon be turning out the lights on our faith tradition in that region. At this point, the superintendent of that United Methodist district spoke up from the back of the room, asking aloud, "So what?"

So what? At first. I experienced this response as a rude interruption; but when I glanced back toward the superintendent, I saw a sparkle in her eye. Then, I realized that she was calling us to claim our faith foundations—to move beyond issues of survival, marketing, and the assumption of institutional value.

So . . . *what?* What would this hypothetical new faith community bring to the people who engaged in it? And what good could it be to the larger world around us, starting in the local zip code and expanding globally? If you have lately seen the difference Christian faith can make in a person's life, it will be easier for your team to articulate the answer to this.

Sometimes we answer "So what?" by means of a value proposition for Christian faith itself. A lot of people today see absolutely no value in going into any church building or finding a "church home." Many are deeply offended by what they do see of church in the public sphere. You are going to have to make a compelling case. The vitality of a warm worship experience will help you make the case. The quality of your kindness and friendship with neighbors will also help make the case. But for all those who haven't been inside a church gathering—or who imagine such a gathering to be boring, offensive, insufficiently masculine, and so on—we had better be able to state its value.

I occasionally ask teams to break into small groups of four and discuss the following questions. I give them fifteen minutes to talk about the first question, and then I give them one new question every ten minutes following, totaling a good hour of conversation. Here are the questions:

- Why Jesus?
- Why church?
- Why this church?
- Why (this new community) here and now?

In the pages ahead, we will explore ways to better understand the people whom we wish to reach and their deepest longings in life. But for now, let us simply acknowledge that we need to offer a compelling *why* that will mobilize the team we are gathering *and* resonate with real, live people in our community. And that same answer for *why* will also undergird our resolve to birth this new worship community if we should grow discouraged in the early months.

3

ASSESSING YOUR
READINESS

Paul Nixon

I n the early years of the twenty-first century, thousands of churches in
the Western world discovered a new burst of life by adding new worship services. Many of those efforts lowered the median age of their
respective congregations and helped to rekindle ministry vitality in some
places where the flame was starting to flicker. Most of the new services
were simpler in format, typically shifting from including a traditional
choir to having a small band of musicians. In many cases, there were
still enough people in the orbit of these churches or with history in these
churches that these new starts thrived. New people began engaging, the
new worship services took root, and total worship attendance rose.

That was then.

Where we used to get 300 attendees on launch day, we are now happy
with 125. Where we used to get 100, we are now sometimes launching with only thirty and working to grow it from there, week by week,
sometimes with surprisingly good results. This is especially true when we
are working with populations that would be identified as living in green
or yellow cultural space in the Spiral Dynamics framework[1]—which
characterizes most adults under the age of forty-five in some areas today.

These populations are likely to be distrustful of organized religion on one hand, while possibly seeing truth as something shared among varied religious traditions on the other. This is not a 1990s American mission field anymore!

A smaller launch-community size is also common when a megachurch or two dominate the local market of individuals and families looking for a church. Even though you may have a significantly different vision than that of the megachurch, it may be hard for you to capture much attention at first: You are probably small starting out, and they are so large, developed, and well designed for spiritual consumers. Remember: Large planets have a lot more gravity than tiny planets!

So, the question of readiness to launch has never been more critical. How do you know if and when your church is ready to do this?

You can start by quickly checking the baseline reasoning among your leadership. The next time you get your team together, simply ask them these two questions:

- Is this new initiative born more out of concern for the population we intend to reach than out of concern for church survival or financial sustainability?
- If we were to succeed at this and reach so many people with the new worship community that they become the majority at our church, swamping the existing leadership boat, would we still want to do this?

If the answer to either of these questions is "No," I can assure you that you are *not ready* to do this. The people you reach will probably quickly catch on to your hesitations or institutionalism and flee the scene. If they don't quickly catch on, there will be conflict later and/or bitter disappointment when the new people who have joined you don't behave like loyal church members from days gone by.

A third question you should ask your church leaders is this:

- Has our church had any success at inviting new people in and helping them to experience a spiritual breakthrough in our midst? In other words, to use a metaphor Jesus loved, do we have any solid experience "catching fish"?

New worship communities are all about catching new fish. And if we don't know how to fish well, we might think first about strengthening our skills before thinking we can land the fish we catch in a boat called *worship*. If our current worship community is ill-suited for the people with whom we want to develop a relationship, we could look to other ministry strategies in the short run—small-group work and community mission engagement (just to name two; there'll be more on this in the pages ahead).

Ten years ago, some of my friends and I developed a self-assessment tool for churches desiring to plant a new ministry for new people. It is called Readiness 360 (www.readiness360.org). More than 1,200 congregations in the US and the UK have taken the assessment. We have normed it across the years, as we correlated the results with church ministry accomplishment in real time. It is a powerfully predictive tool. Today, Phil Maynard of EMC3 Coaching owns Readiness 360. We highly recommend it as a tool for assessing your church's or team's readiness for reaching a multitude of new people. For a modest cost, it will not only show you where you are strong and where you are challenged but it will offer practical tips on how your church might strengthen its ministry readiness to live into its vision. It could save you untold thousands of dollars in spending to launch something that would be doomed from the get-go. Often, churches starting new services are like most third graders cracking open a calculus book, critically lacking in the formative experiences and foundational learning that make calculus accessible and even fun.

Readiness 360 looks at four areas of your church's internal experience or DNA[2]:

1. **Spiritual Intensity**: How robust is people's experience of God in this church, both in terms of personal spiritual practices and in terms of their common life, especially in worship? Is this a church that lives with a high expectancy of what God is about to do next? Are there people or ministries here that we could rightfully describe as being on fire? (This area, as it improves, has been known to rub off on the other three in a positive way.)

2. **Dynamic Relationships**: Does this church have good relational habits among its participants—between leaders and members; between insiders and newcomers; between itself, the neighbors, and other ministry allies; and so on? Churches with healthy relationship patterns; a lack of bullying; good capacity for incorporating new people and their ideas; and strong, authentic hospitality make for places where everyone wants to spend time.

3. **Missional Alignment**: Does this church or launch team know what business it is in? Are leaders able to talk about change and new ideas within the framework of the church's mission, as opposed to simply a matter of personal taste or traditions and habits? Are they able to put some long-running programs or assumptions on sabbatical in order to create capacity (time-wise or financially) for new approaches to ministry more aligned with the church's mission in the current context?[3]

4. **Cultural Openness**: How good is this team at welcoming people who come with a different life narrative than their own, a different cultural history, or a different political or theological perspective? We are finding that the more intercultural experiences people bring before they get to church, the stronger the area of cultural openness may be. Thus, it should not surprise us that many rural or homogeneous churches lag in this category or that younger, urban, highly educated churches are sometimes (although not always) stronger here—perhaps stronger even than in spiritual

intensity. People with military experience may discover an advantage here also, since the military forms extremely diverse people into a very team-dependent community.

If you discern that your church might need to strengthen its readiness before seeking to launch a new worship community, that's great: This will slow down your timeline, and that is no problem at all. God meets us where we are and kindly leads us forward from that point. There is a road of faithfulness for every church and team.

In terms of the four areas above, **here are a few tips on increasing your church's readiness for engaging new people:**

1. **Spiritual Intensity.** This is a core area of church functionality; and as it strengthens, we have noticed that other readiness dimensions are pulled in a good direction. Any emphasis that mobilizes people to increase their day-to-day spiritual practice will offer some benefit not just to those people personally but to their church. Your church could focus on mobilizing everyone to

   - read scripture daily;
   - find a community need and sign up to serve;
   - join a small group that meets at least twice a month to talk about the challenges of living out faith in day-to-day life;
   - take a tithing challenge (perhaps even with a money-back guarantee for those who are scared to try); and
   - commit to a daily rhythm of spiritual practices.

These kinds of actions take a church from being simply a gathering for worship and fellowship and reorient the church as a people who live with a sense of common purpose. In my experience with scores of churches in the last two years, those with high spiritual intensity and clarity of purpose fared much better through the challenges of the pandemic than most.

2. **Dynamic Relationships**. There are two common issues in this area for most churches: First, there is too much solo effort on various ministry chores and tasks and not enough team effort. Volunteering thus becomes tedious and lonely work. Developing stronger teams is often a game-changer. Simply having experience with teamwork will be helpful as a church prepares to tackle the complex task of creating an entirely new worship community. Second, many churches simply do not have experience building relationships with new people. They have seen only a handful of visitors and just a small percentage of those deciding to make the church their home. In some cases, major work is required to help a church learn how to build relationships with new people, even if these new people are not part of a different population niche. In this book, you will find chapter 6 ("Building Bridges with the People We Seek"), chapter 8 ("Developing a Culture of Invitation"), chapter 25 ("Offering World-Class Hospitality"), and chapter 26 ("Onboarding New People into Community") helpful as you think about how to improve your church's interactions with newcomers.

3. **Missional Alignment**. Margaret Brunson[4] reminds me that a particular local church's sense of purpose is likely more specific and more focused than the mission given to God's church for all times and places. In other words, we can't simply pull out the Great Commission, the Great Commandment, or the denominational mission statement and check a box.

I have mixed feelings about the church mission statements I see as I travel. Some mission statements are simply denominational posters, dutifully placed on the bulletin board in the church hallway—no local praying or discernment required. Other mission statements pick up random or peripheral values and seek to make these the flavor of the year in ways that fail to convince me their messages are really at the core of why these churches exist. In these latter cases, the mission statement may simply be what the current management wishes to emphasize. We need clarity about what business our church is in, stated simply in a way that (a) resonates with the core convictions of the people in a place, (b) is relevant to what God is up to in our neighborhood, and (c) is connected to the historic work of the Christian church in all times and places.

Once you have renewed clarity about why your church exists, it is important to audit everything you do and every group that gathers and ask, "How does this activity or group align with the fundamental purpose of this church?" From such clarity, all parts of the church can lean toward the center. An eloquent simplicity may emerge that either aligns or eliminates certain committees or activities. Chapter 1 ("Leading in This Ministry Moment"), chapter 2 ("Why Start a New Gathering?") and chapter 7 ("Developing a Culture of Prayer") may be helpful to your leaders in clarifying the core purpose and calling of your church.

4. **Cultural Openness**. This capacity is mostly related to life experience. It is typically the least developed of the four readiness capacities/areas named here. People with cross-cultural life experience will be helpful on any team that is expected to launch a culturally open ministry. Think in terms of younger people, people who have lived in a variety of places, members of military families, people who have gone to school with or worked with a diverse group of people. Finally, remember that the diversity of the launch team you convene will likely determine the diversity of the community you gather. My 2019 book *Multi: The Chemistry of Church Diversity* may be helpful to you as you think through this challenge and develop a plan. And chapter 18 of this book ("Nurturing Multiethnicity") will likely be helpful to you in this regard, as well.

If your church is not fully ready to start a new ministry that welcomes a wider bandwidth of people into your midst, I recommend that you slow down your plans for establishing the new worship community. Consider spending a year or so strengthening your skills for this challenge. Take the time to do this well. And here's an observation: The churches that most need their leaders to take a few months to sit with scripture and ask, "God, what are you seeking to do through us?" are often the ones most resistant to doing so.

4

NAMING WHAT YOU DO WELL (AND WHAT YOU COULD DO BETTER)

Kim Shockley

In chapter 1, Beth Ann Estock shared how the work of spiritual discernment is critical as you prepare for doing a new thing with God. A part of this discernment is acknowledging what you already do well. It is possible that your congregation has many assets that could have an impact upon how you design and accomplish this new thing well. You always get a bigger ministry "bang" when you align your plans with your assets.

Every church has assets. A church's ministry assets include the following:

- the skills individual people bring to our congregation;
- the passions that arise within the congregation when each person finds ways of serving that bring him or her deep joy;
- the positive attitudes we use to do our work;
- the positive behaviors that help us build authentic, loving relationships with all kinds of people; and
- the reputation and credibility our church may already have in the community as related to certain kinds of ministry.

Some of these assets are intangible, but you also may have some very tangible assets reflected in your congregation's building, staffing, and financial health. Most of us can tick these items off quickly at a meeting—for example, we have *this* much money in the bank, we have *this* number of rooms or spaces that can be used for unique ministry opportunities, or we have *this* staff person who helps us stay focused on what needs to be done. We are used to having conversations around these tangible kinds of assets. But in addition to thinking at this level, I would like to suggest that it is discovering the intangible assets that is the harder—and more critical—preparation work required to do a new thing.

The easiest place to start would be with the skills and passions present within the congregation or within the congregation's reach or network. One way to do this is to list the resources you think you will need to launch a new worship community.[1] For example, you may need the following:

- musicians;
- hospitality personnel, both inside and outside the worship venue;
- worship leaders;
- "set designers" (a modern way of thinking about those who design the worship altar area);
- follow-up contacts for guests and visitors; and
- people to guide the children in spiritual discovery.

When you think about the people within your existing congregation or launch team, who has these skills? Where are the gaps? When you think about the friends and children of members of your existing worship group, who has these skills?

Or you can think in reverse and look first at the skills you are certain your church members have. For example, if your church is in Silicon Valley, you may be blessed with the presence of innovators and engineers who understand the workings of digital community in ways other churches don't. Pay attention to the ways in which your church is distinctively gifted as you move forward.

You might consider administering a two-question survey to mine for the skills and passions that are present within your church. The first question would be something such as, *What skills do you use in your daily life?* The next question, then, would be focused more on passions, such as, *What kinds of activities in your life give you joy?* Such broad, open-ended questions may be just the right tool you need to learn things about your people that you did not know. For example, do you have people (of any age) who consider themselves skilled dancers, organizers, artists, writers, cooks, baristas, cookie bakers, money counters, teachers, trombone players, and so on? Do you have accountants who love playing with their grandchildren, executives who love getting into the kitchen, or retail clerks who love making music in their off-hours? If you find you have skilled artists in your congregation, what kind of experience could they participate in that would help new people glorify God through worship? How could you use teachers or trombone players in a worship experience? I hope you get the idea that designing a worship experience that will make use of the skills the congregation possesses may provide a very different opportunity for interacting with new people, as well as exciting, new opportunities for current church participants that have never been available before.

Beyond the idea of a simple survey, you may notice that some people's eyes sparkle when the topic of starting a new worship community comes up in conversation. Paul Nixon and I talked about this in our book *The Surprise Factor: Gospel Strategies for Changing the Game at Your Church.* Keep a list on your desk of those bright-eyed, energetic people you notice. Pray for them daily. Spend some time with them regularly. Ask God to do God's thing with them, then sit back and see what happens. Be ready to invite these people into leadership and to take seriously their ideas. They may bring something to you that you didn't see or even want. God is doing something through them, so you will find ways to get to *yes* with them, to harness their skills and passions.

Let's shift now, beyond a person's tangible skills and passions, and into the realm of a person's *being*. Skills and passions focus on doing and the energy that drives us in our doing. Ultimately, I believe it is more important to focus on *who we are* than on *what we do*. I can be a great dancer and lead an exciting worship experience. But if I want all the attention for my skill or am a bully to younger dancers, am I the right person to be leading worship? People whose attitudes and behaviors are those of a maturing disciple of Jesus will help you have a more fruitful worship experience, even if their skills need a little more practice and they are relatively young in their faith journey.

What kinds of attitudes and behaviors are we talking about? Let's look at Galatians: "But the fruit of the Spirit is love, joy, peace, forbearance [patience], kindness, goodness, faithfulness, gentleness and self-control. Against such things there is no law" (5:22-23, NIV). These behavioral assets will help your new community thrive and set a positive tone that will mesh with the community's DNA. On the other hand, talent on the team that is not harnessed by the Spirit can run amok and really cause damage.

You might consider developing a relational covenant for your launch team to ensure that the members' behaviors and attitudes function in positive ways as you do your work together. Every individual and every group of human beings has times when things don't go well; so, having an agreed-upon covenant in place in advance will help you navigate through those times. It is much easier to rein in difficult behavior when this work is done first. A process that uses John Wesley's three simple rules[2] is a great model for writing a covenant together. The process is fairly simple:

- List behaviors and attitudes that would do *harm* (such as gossiping, bullying, and so on). Then, ask each person on your team to choose from the list three behaviors they would covenant not to do. Tally the number of votes for each item, and pick the top three vote-getters.

- List behaviors and attitudes that would do *good* (such as practicing respectful conversation, living the agreed-upon values at every level, and so on). Follow the same process as before, with each person on your team choosing from the list three behaviors they would covenant to do. Again, tally the number of votes for each item, and pick the top three.

- List behaviors that help us *stay connected with God* (such as praying daily for the team, reading the same scriptures together, and so on). Then, once again, follow the process for having each group member select three such behaviors from this list, tally the votes, and pick the top three.

Once a covenant is in place and signed by each member of the team, make sure you review it every time you meet for the first few weeks, and then at least once a month thereafter. Revisiting your covenant will help the team remember its worth and its high calling. At every meeting, ask, "What do we celebrate about having the covenant in place? What are our concerns about living this covenant? What do I need to confess?"

Another way to answer the question "What are we really good at?" is to find out what the neighborhood around the church thinks about the congregation: What is [Anytown] Church really known for by its neighbors, especially those who do not attend any of its functions? What is its reputation on the community grapevine? What do you want that reputation to be? Is there a match between what actually is and what is desired? Taking a two-question survey of random people, you could simply ask, *Have you ever heard of [Anytown] Church? What is the first thing that comes to mind when you think of them?*

Discovering the congregation's reputation can be sobering work, but it is essential in navigating toward something new. Nearly every church has some kind of misstep in its history that has soured some of its neighbors. These negative feelings could be related simply to people's public perceptions of organized religion in general or to the denominational brand of the church. What specific assets does your church possess (or can your church develop) to overcome a negative reputation?

A few years ago, a growing, progressive Baptist church in Washington, DC, discovered that *Baptist* equates with *the Religious Right* in the minds of many Washingtonians. So, the leadership of this church added a tagline to their name: *A different kind of Baptist*. Similarly, a downtown United Methodist congregation in Texas, one with a reputation as "a gathering for rich folks," began a campaign: *We love (Name of Their City)*. They worked hard for years to live up to that tagline and to teach their neighbors that they cared deeply about the whole city and all its residents.

Everyone in the church should be aware that how they talk about the life of their congregation—its members and its leaders—matters deeply. Leaders should exercise care especially in regard to how they speak of their church in public; this is even more imperative when there is controversy of some sort. By focusing on the good news, we can help other people see that God is active in our community. Remember, the witness of people to their community happens whenever they talk about what is happening in the life of their church and their own faith opportunities. This witness can be both positive and negative, so always pay attention to maximizing the positive in public at all times.

In summary, there are things you are good at. We all need to take seriously those gifts in our ministry visioning and planning and recognize that there are things we need to get better at in order to be ready for the ministry challenges before us.

5

FOCUSING ON A PARTICULAR SET OF PEOPLE

Matt Temple

It was our thirteenth trip to the emergency room within a period of three months. These trips never took place at convenient times. Typically, we were making our way to the hospital at hours when most people are nestled quietly in their beds. My wife, Angie, had some stomach issues that we thought had been addressed in a successful procedure; but shortly after the procedure, a different set of problems began. She would have bouts of intense pain in her abdomen that would not subside. The majority of our trips were to the same hospital, so that when we walked through the doors, we should have expected a bit of understanding as to who she was, why we were there (yet again), and what tests had previously been done to try to diagnose the issue. Yet each time we arrived, Angie was forced to go through the same procedures, as if it were our first trip, and endure hours of excruciating pain. There were no notes readily available giving hospital staff background information or access to her previous medical records. So, on each visit, we would go through the same two hours of the emergency-room protocol before the hospital staff would call Angie's doctor and try to find a real solution. Each time, she would attempt to describe what was going on and the intense pain. And each time, we would explain to them exactly what we knew they were going to do over the next two hours; but our explanations were to no avail. *There are few things more frustrating than not being heard.*

We live in a world fixated on efficiency. We look for similarities (and many times assume them), and then we find ways to streamline for what we hope will provide the greatest impact with the least amount of resources. Far too often, our efficiency obsession also affects how we imagine and practice ministry. But making the gospel meaningful for a particular context is rarely an exercise in efficiency. Too often, our church, much like our local emergency room, may try to create solutions for a people they know little to nothing about; we answer questions no one is asking and then wonder why nobody feels compelled to come.

In Lewis Carroll's *Alice's Adventures in Wonderland,* Alice comes to a fork in the road and is met by her curious friend the Cheshire Cat. She asks the cat, "Would you tell me, please, which way I ought to go from here?" To which the Cheshire Cat responds, "That depends a good deal on where you want to get to." Alice, still trying to find her bearings in this strange world, tells her mysterious guide that she does not know or really care. To which the Cheshire Cat responds, "Then it doesn't matter which way you go."[1]

The same is true for us in seeking to design something new. Our design process will be filled with forks in the road where we must make critical strategic decisions. Yet like some of the emergency room staffs my wife and I encountered, we often neglect to really see and listen to the people we are seeking to reach. Instead, we start thinking about what it is we need to do and how we need to do it. When we don't pay serious attention to those we wish to reach, we may just start designing randomly, as though the processes we follow and the actions we take really don't matter: "Another church did *this;* that sounds cool!" And so on. This results in disconnection from the very people we seek to affect.

As we enter the visioning process for launching a new worship community, we should take the time necessary to understand the people for whom we are designing this ministry:

- Who are we designing this for?
- Why them?
- How have we experienced God leading us toward this population?

And beyond the question of who, what will it take for us to deeply understand their life experiences and aspirations? A deeper question still: How are we falling in love with this population and coming to feel empathy for them?

Then, only when we have identified and empathized with the people we seek to reach should we dive into innovation and the creative genius that exists in us all to craft the experience appropriately. If we are not listening to and learning from the people we are called to reach, then we must ask ourselves whether this new project is about building *our* kingdom or *God's* kingdom.

Good Design Work Begins at the Intersection of Empathy and Creativity

Empathy is about developing an understanding for what another person feels and experiences. In Matthew 9:36, we are told that Jesus saw those gathered around him and observed in them a longing. This observation led Jesus to have compassion. The word *compassion* in this text means "to feel with." Jesus' observation led to a deeper understanding that ultimately led to empathy. It was out of this empathy that Jesus' creative genius met the people right where they were.

Going into our design process, it is likely that we have at least a general idea about the people we are designing the worship experience for. It is important that we identify and describe these initial internal assumptions, but we must also align those assumptions with the reality of who lives around us. Within the world of anthropology (the study of human society and culture), there are generally three ways to "see" the people in a certain context or study area. The three observation strategies are the following:

- nonparticipant/indirect observation;
- nonparticipant/direct observation; and
- participant observation.

Each of these three strategies has benefits, and each of the three is necessary. These strategies move along a spectrum, from limited immersion to maximum immersion. Often, the more immersive the experience, the more uncomfortable it is for us, as it takes us into situations where we are asked to be the guest and not the host. However, the more immersed we become, the more likely it is that empathy and clarity will develop.

Let's look at this through this lens of baseball. As a baseball fan, *nonparticipant/indirect observation* happens when I follow the statistics of my favorite players and team. I don't actually have to watch a game to see some of the trends and understand what is happing with the team. Through looking at batting statistics, winning percentage, swing and miss rates, and thousands of other data points, I can draw some high-level conclusions. However, all this data must move through my own interpretive lens; and, consequently, the story the data tells me will be very limited and subjective.

This leads to *nonparticipant/direct observation*. In our baseball analogy, this happens when I watch as many games as possible. With this strategy, the closer I am to the game, the better my ability will be to interpret the story the data is telling me about who the players are. I could watch the games on TV, but, ideally, I would be present in the stadium to take in the whole immersive experience. Even though this method gets me closer to the real story of the players, it still keeps me at a distance.

The best way for me to truly understand the players would be through *participant observation*. This would require me to somehow become a participant in the games being played. I could do this by becoming an umpire; a coach; or, if I had the gifts for it, a player on the team. It would require spending time on baseball fields and in dugouts, experiencing all sorts of situations with the players.

In starting a new worship community, nonparticipant/indirect observation could happen through studying census reports, blogs, local news outlets, travel patterns, Facebook community pages, and/or Nextdoor,[2] as well as looking at data organizations such as MissionInsite[3] or Gloo.[4] This is the least immersive of the observation strategies. It will give us high-level, general information about the people living in a particular context or geographic region and can help our team begin to identify and clarify whom we are designing the worship experience for.

With *nonparticipant/direct observation*, we are looking less at data and more at behavior within a particular environment. We are likely bringing with us some hypotheses and assumptions about the people to whom we feel called and are now looking to confirm our hypotheses. Some would call this ethnographic research. We do this simply by being consistently present in people's context and observing their behavior. This could take place at a coffee shop, a local park, a sporting event, and so on. Other ways we can engage people in nonparticipant/direct observation would include through surveys and by having one-to-one conversations.

Finally, in *participant observation*, we discover where the people we have identified as our target currently gather, and we participate in those spaces to make connections, build relationships, and gain a deeper understanding and empathy. Through this immersive experience, we may consider inviting the people we meet into our design process. We can give them the opportunity to speak into what would be a meaningful worship experience for them.

In participant observation, we are able to move beyond demographic data and understand who people are internally: *Why do they do what they do? What motivates them, inspires them, gives them a sense of meaning?* The questions to which we might seek answers regarding these people can expand to include the following:

- What do they value?
- What are they afraid of?
- What concerns occupy their minds?
- How do they make sense of the world?
- What questions are they asking?
- What are their rhythms; what are the patterns for how they spend their time?
- What is the makeup of their relational circle?
- What fills their free time?
- What do they dream about?
- What brings them joy? What do they celebrate?

True empathy requires a connection—a shared concern and a relationship. Identifying who it is we believe to be our chosen audience for our new ministry requires us to move beyond transactional connections to genuine relationships. It means challenging our assumptions and moving out of our own comfort zones so we can truly listen to and understand the people we believe God is calling us to reach. For white persons, it also means letting go of our own colonial instinct and the residue that worldview has left on our theological framework. In this way, we are better able to approach the people we believe God has called us to from a posture of humble servanthood. We can be intentional in choosing to listen and seek to understand so that we can communicate and embody the grace of God in a way that is compelling and meaningful within the local context.[5]

6

BUILDING BRIDGES WITH THE PEOPLE WE SEEK

Kay Kotan

In the previous chapter, Matt Temple prompted us to think about whom we are seeking to reach. Too often, we try to reach everyone, and, therefore, we reach no one. Or we try to reach a population that does not live in the neighborhood we are called to serve. It is important to first do the work of identifying *whom*, exactly, we are seeking to reach before we move into the ministry of identifying *how* we will reach this focus population. This is not only important work but also holy work. Through it, we are saying, "This is whom we are taking responsibility to reach for Jesus; these are the souls we will take responsibility for."

As we get a clearer picture of the people we are trying to reach, we must become experts in knowing these people deeply. Of course, we will need to know their age span, life stages, typical occupations, family statuses, types, and sizes, and income levels—the sort of demographic information that is readily available. But we will also need to go deeper: What keeps these folks up at night? What are they celebrating? What are they worried about? What are their stressors? What do they like to do with their leisure time? How do they prefer to receive information and communicate? How do they feel about spirituality? religion? politics?

What organizations do they support? What organizations do they belong to? What are their goals and aspirations?

We cannot assume any of this information. We need to investigate and ask! We cannot assume that last year's data is still valid this year, especially if something as life-altering as a pandemic roars through. Furthermore, we need to make sure we think beyond our own personal preferences. Too often, we think we know our neighbors, and we make assumptions about our neighbors, but our assumptions turn out to be way off base. This is especially true if we do not live in the neighborhood, have not lived in the neighborhood for more than a couple of years, and/or do not "do life" in the neighborhood. It is also true if we are not a part of the focus demographic for the new worship community. In short, a group of church people cannot sit in a circle in the fellowship hall and magically figure answers out.

There are a variety of ways to become expert in knowing our neighbors. Keep in mind, this will be an ongoing process. We live in an ever-changing world, so we will need to keep up-to-date on the information that pertains to them continually by identifying changes in trends and demographics. This can best be done when we are a part of the community we are trying to reach. If we do not live among the population we are seeking to reach, then hopefully, several members of our team do. Planting a new worship community is not a one-person job. It is not a pastor-only job. It is the ongoing work of a team.

In chapter 5, Matt Temple mentioned some good sources of demographic information. With regard to MissionInsite, be sure to look at the information specific to your targeted demographic or focus population. It is not enough simply to look at overall population trends in your neighborhood. There are multiple Mosaic segments identified in each MissionInsite report that enable a deeper dive into discovering information about your focus population. Mosaic segment information can tell you about where a particular demographic likes to travel or what media they prefer to watch, along with the type of leisure activities they enjoy, just to name a few. MissionInsite also has reports called Ministry Insights and Religious Insights that reveal what your neighborhood residents think about organized religion and what type of ministry or other programs they may find to be of value. You will, of course, need to test this information through real-life conversations. These sorts of tools are invaluable, and they can give you a big head start as you seek to identify and understand your focus population on a deeper level.

This data will provide you with some tips about your neighbors that you then can test out in real-life conversations and through exploration. You must get out to be with the people you are trying to reach in order to really get to know them. Matt referred to this as "participant information"; I refer to it as walk-around information. Set out with a heightened sense of curiosity about the focus population: What makes them tick? What ticks them off? What amuses them? People love to talk about themselves and tell their stories; *ponder their stories*. Ask lots of questions. Hold some community-focus groups with your focus population. Walk around with a clipboard in front of a grocery store and give people a gift card for a free cup of coffee if they will talk to you for five minutes. You will be amazed at what you can learn. If you develop and sustain an ongoing mission or ministry project with your neighbors, people may begin to hang out together after the tasks are completed. Whenever people are lingering after a project or an event just to hang out, please, stay and hang out—listen and learn!

As you learn more about your focus population, you will, of course, be seeking to build bridges with them relationally. How do you do this? You use the information you have learned through the varied means above. Community will build naturally around the needs, desires, and passions of the focus population.

Here is an example. Let's say that your focus population has a certain passion for making a difference in the life of their community. In conversation with them, you discover common ground regarding the desire to revitalize a city park in the neighborhood. This passion becomes the cause. You then build a community around this cause in order to provide a solution. Someone from the church partners up with someone from the community. Together, you build a small team. The team gathers to develop a strategy. The team then begins to build partnerships within the community and build upon the passion, with more coming from the focus population. A rally day occurs, where an active group of people come together to begin repairs and beautification for the park, in partnership with the city, the church, and nearby businesses. Work teams are organized for future work, through which names are exchanged and relationships are built. Soon, different parts of the community are intersecting on a routine basis at the park. The launch team for your new worship service is involved in all of this, hanging out and building relationships with the work teams and community partners. The new worship service launches in the city park, where you all celebrate how you have come together around your shared passion through this cause, and you begin to decide what beautification project you will pursue together next.

Here is another example. This time, the demographic information and conversations reveal to you that your focus population is made up of single twenty- and thirty-something adults who are looking for community. They are busy starting careers or holding fast-track corporate positions, working many hours each week. Relationships are difficult to build, they find, especially since few in this focus population are "from here" originally. Your research finds that the majority of this focus population's members use Instagram as their preferred social media channel. Their areas of high passion and interest include travel and craft beer. So, you develop a set of Instagram posts (hopefully vetted by a marketing person who is a member of the same focus population) for a new community group of twenty- and thirty-something professionals interested in travel to meet at the local craft beer establishment. The group can meet new people and make new friends with the same interests, share travel stories, and sample the local craft beer together.

You get the idea. We meet people where they are, doing what they like to do. The times when people were specifically looking for a church or automatically coming to us are over. We must become missionaries in our own neighborhoods and build authentic relationships with people first in order to build trust with them, most likely before they will ever want to be part of a church community with us.

When I am trying to reach new people to launch a new worship service, new church, or new group, I like to think about relationship-building as a three-pronged approach:

- The first prong is your personal, one-on-one relationships. How are you going about your daily life? Are you slowing down long enough to notice and meet new people, be friendly, and offer blessings? Too often, we are in such a rush that we put on blinders, and we don't even notice the people around us. Who is one new person you are trying to get to know in this season and build a relationship with, so that you might have the opportunity to share your faith story? As a disciple, we are called to be disciple makers.
- The second prong is what I refer to as the "elbow approach" or small-group approach. For example, think about your neighbors. Do you know all of them? How about your coworkers? Too often, we do not know the people around us. Gather your neighbors for a neighborhood barbecue, a concert, or board games to build relationships. As churched folks, we often spend all of our time hanging out with other churched folks and not expanding our relationship circles. Our views of the world become limited and perhaps even skewed, as we become more and more disconnected from the very people we are called to reach for Jesus.
- The third prong is what I refer to as bridge events. While the first prong is one-on-one and the second is through the framework of

a small group, this prong is an all-church event. A bridge event is for the sole purpose of building relationships with those who are unchurched. It should be a "*P*-Free Zone": No Preaching, No Prayers, No Pressure, and No Pocketbooks. A bridge event should be held outside the church walls and, preferably, not on the church grounds. The idea is to create a safe, comfortable, and nonthreatening space where the unchurched people in your focus population can have a good time and where you can all begin to build authentic relationships with one another.

There are some caveats for carrying out well done bridge events. They are not hard to do, but you must clearly identify the purpose of the event, the intended outcomes, and the plans for follow-up. For example, who will be the members of the team that will write personal notes and follow up through personal contacts after the event to continue to build relationships with those who attended? Also, a prayer team needs to be in place behind the scenes. While there is no public prayer for a bridge event, it should be bathed in prayer from beginning to end. Understand that if you can't get a prayer team together to support the bridge event, you are not ready to have the event or launch a new worship service.

Often at an event, we will have all of the volunteers who are on hand assigned to various "tasks." However, we also forget that the most important job at any bridge event is to extend radical hospitality: Who is connecting with the guests, learning their names, spending time visiting with them, and building relationships? Sometimes we are so busy pulling off the event—grilling hotdogs, running logistics, and so on—that we unintentionally ignore our guests. We must remember the *Why* of the event: The purpose of a bridge event is to build relationships, so this should remain our primary focus.[1]

Bridges are two-way transport systems across a body of water or a ravine, facilitating passage that would otherwise be impossible. But too often in the church, we treat these transport systems as if they were one-way, expecting the community to travel across the bridge to *us*, the church. The community may see the bridge to the church as impassable for them, due to all the baggage (such as hurts, hypocrisies, pain, and postmodern assumptions) clogging up their traffic lanes. To be the church of tomorrow, we need to think about the bridge as being two-way: First, we walk out of the church, across the bridge, and into the community to build intentional, authentic relationships with the people there. Second, we walk across the bridge, elbow-to-elbow, back to the church with our new friends to introduce them to Jesus. Then, we can go back across the bridge together, back into the community, to meet more people where they are, build more relationships, and find the opportunities to introduce them to Jesus.

In the next three chapters, we will look at dimensions of the community culture that are essential in a thriving church—prayer, invitation, and community engagement. The DNA of thriving churches will vary from one to the next, depending on issues of culture and God's call, but these three chapters will focus on habits of life that should be universal. The earlier we establish these habits in the life of our new faith community, the more likely they will strengthen that community and allow it to become a conduit of blessing to a whole host of people.

7

DEVELOPING A CULTURE
OF PRAYER

Bener Agtarap

Starting a new faith community is a daunting task. We see that planters are facing more challenges these days than before. Living out our call to connect new people with the love of God in Jesus can be overwhelming. Some of these challenges are minor in nature and can be resolved within a short period of time. Other challenges are more serious and significant, placing a lot of pressure and burden on leaders and planting teams, making it difficult to move forward with confidence and function in a healthy way.

Although planting a new faith community is never easy, church planting is one of the most exciting and rewarding experiences for me—and for many others—in life. I would do it again in a heartbeat.

I planted my first church in Manila, in the Philippines, as a layperson in 1984. I had limited training, almost no experience, and very little support from my denomination. I encountered multiple challenges that I had no idea how to handle. Over time, I discovered three universal issues that I and other planters around the world face each day: becoming overworked, overwhelmed, and tired. This triple blow can knock us out.

What do we need to do to stay active and involved in church planting? The best way to stay in the game is to stay connected with a real and reliable source of strength, peace, and hope: God. And the way to connect with God is through prayer. I don't know how I could ever survive a spiritual startup without being intentional in my prayer life. Jesus knew that he needed to stay connected with God. He prayed, day and night, as an essential part of his routine. The disciples saw what prayer did for Jesus, and they asked him to teach them how to pray (see Matthew 6:5-15; Mark 11:25; Luke 11:1-13). If you are planting a new ministry, I encourage you to learn to pray as Jesus taught his disciples.

What did the disciples see in Jesus that made them think prayer could help them deal with the challenges they were facing? Did they think prayer would help them be more like Jesus and, therefore, more like God? How did they see prayer benefiting them amid challenges? Here is my best guess: As the disciples started facing some challenges in following Jesus, they simply realized that they needed more than what they had and what they could do as human beings, both individually and corporately.

As we engage in launching a new thing, let's ask Jesus to teach us to pray also, as he taught his first followers. Jesus began with God. Jesus began his earthly ministry by journeying out into the wilderness to pray. He did not start his ministry in public squares, performing miracles, teaching, preaching, healing the sick, or eating with sinners. Jesus inaugurated his mission work with prayer. This not only gave him strength but also helped him to discern and stay focused on the particular directions in which God was leading him.

As an avid pool player, I can tell you that winning in billiards (or simply enjoying the game) begins with training and preparation. As a new grandfather of a beautiful granddaughter, I can testify that preparation for taking this little creature for her first ride in the car is vital to an enjoyable trip. As a seasoned church planter, I can boldly say that prayer is the most significant preparation for the work of launching a new faith community.

As you think or dream about launching a new worship community for new people, you have to ask yourself: *How is this part of God's vision? How can this new thing better serve the mission of God in bringing more people to God's love? How can I get myself and my team ready to launch it?* Spending time in prayer will certainly help you answer some of these questions. As you continually pray for this new thing, you will find clarity in your reasons for doing it, and you will be more ready to pursue it with inner hope and resilience. In many cases these days, planters are trying new strategies and even reimagining church for a new context. Such innovation rightly starts with the Holy Spirit, and prayer is a critical means for how we discover the new things God wishes to do.

As you began planning how to live into God's vision of a new worship community, you started thinking about some creative ways of connecting with people and getting them excited for this vision. You have been seeking to form relationships. While you are thinking about these different relationships, you also likely are spending a substantial amount of time thinking about systems and structures—setting goals, securing funding, and so on. Former church planter Junius Dotson has a word of advice for consideration. He writes in his book *Soul Reset*, "I'd quickly learn that balancing the institutional demands and the pure desire of wanting people to meet Jesus would prove a tricky task. The more I walked the line between those two goals, the more stressed and overwhelmed I became."[1] If you are at this same critical point on your journey, it may be a good time to call for a time-out. Go for several days to a place somewhere away from your planting world. Find a place, and create time to be fully present with God. Invite your spouse or partner in ministry to pray with you. At some point, after you return, you will also need to pray with the members of your launch team. Pray unceasingly.

At age thirty-three (after spending ten years as a local pastor), I was appointed by my bishop to serve as the district superintendent of United Methodist churches in the southwestern area of metropolitan Manila.

Bishop Emerito Nacpil asked me to launch an aggressive missional strategy for creating a new district in the province of Cavite, southwest of Manila. At that time, I already had seven new churches planted under my leadership, so I was fairly confident in the business of planting new faith communities. However, the idea of creating a new district in a new mission field was a big deal. This assignment was much bigger than what I thought I could accomplish as the lead person. If there is one thing that really made me stay in the mission, it is prayer. After six years of hard work, Cavite District was organized with fifty-eight new United Methodist churches, fueled by the power of prayer.

There are five things I would like for you to remember:

- **Understand that you are doing something for God**. You are the leader, but you are receiving your marching orders from God. Staying in touch with God through prayer will give you the stamina you need to hang in there, even amid opposition and roadblocks. In everything you do and at all points along the journey of church planting, make sure you do it as a faithful expression of your prayerful connection with God.

- **Making prayer a priority will lead you to accomplish greater results—often beyond your plans, your goals, and your imagination.** Rachel Gilmore and her new church in Virginia were transitioning from meeting in a theater to their first leased space, and all predictions said the move would lead to a decline in the life of the plant. As they renovated their new space, church members gathered three times a week to pray and paint their way through the process. When they launched worship in their new location, they noticed that their numbers had grown by more than 20 percent. The church plant celebrated and attributed their growth to the power of prayer.

- **Prayer is the work of the whole congregation**. The people of Bupyeong Methodist Church believe in this principle. It is no wonder why this church grew to be one of the largest Protestant churches in South Korea. In his testimony, Rev. Eun-Pa Hong tells us that keeping prayer at the center of congregational life is key to the vitality and growth of this church. It is their practice to pray for a significant number of days, accompanied by fasting for forty days, before they embark on any types of ministries or projects, whether it's a multimillion-dollar building project or supporting a startup congregation in India. Every day, 365 days a year, an average of 400 to 500 people come to the church sanctuary at five o'clock in the morning to pray. They believe that without prayer, they can't do anything but that everything is possible through the power of prayer.

- **Quieting yourself will help you maintain your focus on your mission.** I got involved in campus ministry in college. One of the spiritual practices of our group was what they called "quiet time." This was a designated time for reading scripture and listening to God through prayer. The discipline required is to be quiet so you can clearly hear God's voice through the inspiration of the scripture and the Spirit. Any time you launch a new ministry, there will be constant challenges. It is very easy to become distracted and lose focus on the mission. After a long day or week of doing ministry, there will be exhaustion; frustration; and sometimes even confusion. Prayer itself will not fix all your problems at once. But when you quiet yourself before God through prayer, you can have a more realistic approach to solving your problems; you can have the humility to accept failures as opportunities to mature in faith and in your leadership; you are able to welcome criticism with an open mind and a willingness to be better; and your actions become an expression of the will of God, which is of the utmost importance.

- **Pray in the times of joy and not just when you feel the struggle.** Church planting is not all about hardships or challenges. It also brings much joy to everyone involved. A few years ago, my wife and I, along with two of our family friends, started a new faith community in the living room of our house in Sacramento, California. As we grew in numbers, we moved our gathering place to the ground floor of the United Methodist conference center in West Sacramento. There are so many great stories I could tell about this new church, but the one memory that stands out most is when we welcomed a single mother and her son to join our church. Bishop Warner Brown administered the sacrament of baptism and received them as members of the whole Christian community. In unison, our church leaders and congregation lifted up our prayer of praise and thanksgiving to God. With every single victory in the life of this new church, we prayed with great thanksgiving. Praying together for God's blessings, small or large, continually reminds us that this new community is God's creation.

In prayer, we connect ourselves to the heart of God and to the way God is moving in our time. And from there, we move to our task of connecting all God's children to Jesus, who is the perfect revelation of God's love.

8

DEVLOPING A CULTURE
OF INVITATION

Kim Griffith

I began writing this chapter in January of 2020, when none of us could imagine that church buildings would soon be closed for many months to come. Now, as we have experienced the church's response to the worldwide COVID-19 pandemic, we have learned that we can create a culture of invitation, even when we aren't meeting in person. Whether we are asking people to join us in person or to connect digitally, the reason for our invitation remains constant: We want to introduce our friends and family to Jesus Christ. We want to invite them into a community where they can find a place to call home and be a part of transforming their neighborhood and the world.

Inviting people to church has become a more complicated endeavor in the twenty-first century. Frankly, we are not very good at it. United Methodist Bishop Bob Farr calculates that in The United Methodist Church, the average church member invites someone to church once every thirty-eight years. (Yes, you read that correctly.) So, what is it that makes extending an invitation so difficult? In particular, what is so difficult about inviting someone to join us in something that has been so instrumental in our own lives?

The pandemic unveiled some interesting trends. Churches with an in-person attendance of forty, fifty, or one hundred were suddenly seeing their numbers double and triple when they moved to online worship. In conversations with pastors and church members, we discovered that many found it easier to invite people to watch an online service than to ask them to come to the church in person. Posting a link to a service, hosting virtual watch parties, and connecting friends virtually with their churches opened the door to invitations that might never have happened in person.

As we consider what our invitation will be to our friends and neighbors, we need to use all the options available to us. We can leverage the online space that affords us the ability to invite from a distance, and we can also learn how to share our story in person with friends and neighbors.

In Crafting Your Invitation, Keep These Key Things in Mind

First, invitations are all about relationships. People will come to check out a new worship community because they have met the pastor and like his or her vision for the church or because they have a preexisting relationship with someone there. These relationships create a bridge to the community. Our initial invitation comes out of our desire to share the value we have found in the worship community with others who matter to us. Often, we will discover that persons we invite will come because of our invitation and stay because they fall in love with the community. Ultimately, the love they witness between members of the worship community is the thing that connects them to Christ.

In chapter 3, Paul Nixon mentioned that shortcuts are killing us. This is a critical point to remember about building relationships. To create safe spaces to extend invitations, we must first do the work of building relationships and trust with the people in our circles. As you think about the people you interact with on a regular basis—family, friends, neighbors, coworkers, your nail tech, your barber, your Zumba class members, and so on—you will want to begin to develop a story/narrative about your own faith and about this new faith community that you believe would appeal to them. In the past, most often, people who came to church had been raised in the church or had become a Christian and then found a church to attend. Today, people connect with new faith communities for a variety of reasons and with a diverse set of experiences or perceptions of church. Understanding their personal narrative and experience of the church (or the lack thereof) can help you share parts of your own story that will be the most helpful for them.

To meet people where they are and respect their perception of church, ask yourself the following questions:

1. Do they identify as Christian?
2. Did they grow up in the church?
3. Have they experienced judgment or difficulty with the church in the past?
4. What is their general perception of the church?
5. What is the greatest need in their life right now related to connecting with a community?

Second, craft your story. Think back to chapter 2, "Why Start a New Gathering?" Consider your answers to the following questions:

1. Why are you starting this new faith community?
2. Why are you excited to be a part of this new thing?
3. Why would I want to spend time hanging out at church with you?
4. Will I fit in and feel welcome?
5. [*If you aren't the pastor*] What is the pastor like?

Using your answers to these questions to craft a story will help you be prepared when opportunities present themselves to share about your new faith community. People generally love to hear stories about what is important to you; the more you can share how your life has been blessed and/or transformed by this community, the more likely others will be interested.

Once you start sharing your story, you may be surprised by the results. One of the most interesting church-invitation experiences that I have had happened to me when I moved to a new neighborhood. I was getting a manicure, and I asked the nail technician if she went to church anywhere near the neighborhood. She replied that she was not a Christian, but that one of her clients was always sharing incredibly inspiring stories about her church and the good things they did for the community. The nail technician then took out her cell phone, called this client, told her that she had met someone who was looking for a good church, and asked her to tell me about her church. Then, the technician handed me the phone. Suddenly, I was talking with a woman about her church, and she was inviting me to visit. Since this woman was so excited about her church and willing to share her stories with people, she had inspired a non-Christian woman to connect people to her church.

Thinking through and writing your answers to the questions above and becoming comfortable sharing your stories about your church will ensure that you are prepared to plant seeds of interest that can lead to invitations. While this may seem like far more work than simply asking someone to come to church with you, it creates an atmosphere of trust that enables you to genuinely connect with people. Unfortunately, the church has a public-relations problem. Many churches today find themselves on the wrong side of history in regard to their positions on various social issues and questions. It is up to us to dispel the doubt or fear that our friends, family, and acquaintances may have about connecting with our church. It may be important for us to show that our church is markedly different from many other churches. For those who have little or no experience with church, they may have an image of church based on what they see portrayed in the news. While churches do incredible outreach to their communities, sadly, the images often amplified in the news are of the churches who are calling people names, supporting racist politicians, and/or telling others that they are going to hell. When we share the stories of our communities and the incredible, life-changing love and grace we experience within the church and through our faith, we begin to change the narrative of what some people may assume about church and Christians.

Third, practice sharing your story. In order to be comfortable and prepared to share parts of your story with friends, neighbors, and people in your community, you need to practice sharing your story. You will not share the same exact version of your story in every situation or with every person. For example, you will have a longer version of your story that you may share with your family and your close friends; they already trust you, and they will likely be more open to listening to why this new faith community is important to you and why you want to share it with them. For acquaintances, neighbors, and coworkers, you may have less time to share your story, and they may be less open to invitation. This is where crafting short vignettes out of your answers to the questions above is important. When you take opportunities, over the course of time, to share quick stories, you build trust and interest. Once people realize you are sharing about something important to you (rather than trying to proselytize them), they will be more receptive to listening. And over time, if they are interested in knowing more, they will then feel comfortable asking you for more information.

Fourth, find and create opportunities to share your story. Once you have crafted your story about how your faith (or faith community) is important to you and the ways it has affected your life, consider the variety of interactions you have in your day-to-day life as opportunities to connect. Just as the woman in the nail salon used her conversations with her nail tech to share the feeling of excitement about her church, so too can you have similar conversations every day. Make a list of places where you interact with others on a regular basis; places such as work, school, the gym, your hair salon, the neighborhood pool, your favorite coffee shop, and anywhere else you spend your time should be included. Then, think about at least one person in each place whom you hope to connect with over the next few months. Every person you connect with may not be open to an invitation to attend church; but some of them may connect you with a friend who is, and then, at the very least, you will have made a new friend in your neighborhood.

Ultimately, the goal of starting a new faith community is to reach new people and connect them with Christ. The new community will never become reality without people inviting other people. This is our most important task. Creating a culture of invitation means that each person in the faith community is expected to be sharing his or her story and inviting people to connect not only at the beginning but throughout the life of the church. There is always someone new we can invite. Make a regular practice of asking people to share the first names of the people they are hoping to invite. Collectively praying over their names will remind everyone that the Holy Spirit is already at work, preparing their hearts.

Whether online or in person, take the time to sit down one-on-one with the people in your life whom you hope to connect with your new faith community. Take the first step by sharing your story and begin building a bridge to an invitation!

9

DEVELOPING A CULTURE OF COMMUNITY ENGAGEMENT

Paul Nixon

In the previous two chapters, my friends Bener Agtarap and Kim Griffith focused on two key habits in the life of a thriving faith community: prayer and invitation. I have *never* seen a new worship community planted well without a strong prayer dynamic. I have *rarely* seen a new worship community thrive without a lot of inviting going on.

But I have coached a few planting pastors who prayed constantly, and still their churches could not get off the ground. And I have watched many teams seek to rally members to invite, yet little or no inviting ever happened. In these instances, there was almost always a missing piece: I would call this missing piece *community engagement*. Kim's husband, Jim Griffith, often calls church planting "a contact sport." But if there is inadequate engagement with the local population, the people of the church may have trouble making contact with the folks who would be blessed to share in a new faith community.

Every time I stumble onto a fun new series on Netflix or Amazon, I can't keep quiet about it. It is normal to buzz about the things in life that give us joy. Yet when it comes to church, the buzzing often stops—especially for longtime church participants. I have observed in a variety of cultures that the longer people have been part of a church, the less likely it is that they invite anyone in their lives to share in it.

They may be prayerful, spiritually grounded people. And they may love the idea of their church reaching new people. They might even be willing to invite a friend, if, indeed, they could think of someone to invite. But they can't think of anyone. Often, people who have been inside churches for decades choose for themselves friends who have also been inside churches for decades. Or perhaps they have some friends with whom their friendship is built around something other than religious affinity. In the latter case, they may not want to jeopardize a friendship by inserting religion into the mix.

The solution is to greatly increase the number of people with whom we are rubbing elbows in the larger community. In other words, we have to get out of the church building and beyond the church circles and really dive into community! Churches whose members make lots of friends and allies will discover that great relationships always go *somewhere*.

When a team plants a new worship community out of a large, well-established mother church, it easy to bank on internal church relationships and momentum and take a shortcut past the necessary community relationship development. A well-established church is often like a large planet with a strong force of gravity. It has enough weight and visibility that most people in the community may know about it. It can attract a steady stream of new people simply through good community presence, both online and with its ministry programming. Because of this, the planting team may just be counting on their church's momentum and community visibility to do the inviting for them. Let me be clear: In a new launch, the farther the new community is geographically or culturally from the mother church, the more intentional relationship development and community collaboration must be! Most new worship communities cannot plant as if they were megachurches. You may read certain how-to books or watch certain YouTube channels, and it looks so easy; but you likely do not have a megachurch's volume of people or their community visibility.

In chapter 6, Kay Kotan taught us about sponsoring bridge events—gatherings and projects that engage the population around us, creating a bridge across which new folks can walk, coming closer to relationship with the people in the worship community. But in many cases, churches have not invested enough in the community to find many people ready to walk across any bridge.

A church near Baltimore wanted to take their annual church picnic and turn it into a community event, for the purpose of neighboring. This, in itself, was commendable. They moved the grills, the picnic tables, and the inflatable bouncy house from the church's back yard to its front yard, so that the neighbors could see everything and feel welcomed. The church members went from house to house in the neighborhood, putting out flyers and doorknob hangers advertising the picnic. And that first year of this new community event, sixteen people attended from outside the church membership. However, in year two, the church neglected distributing the doorknob hangers, and no community residents attended other than church members. The church people then decided, "We tried this, and it just didn't work."

I met with the church's leaders and was surprised that absolutely no one from the community had come. I pushed a bit: "Not even with a big, bright bouncy house in the front yard?" They replied, "No." So, I asked, "What's up with the neighbors?" To which one woman responded with a tense edge in her voice, "They're all on drugs." I pondered that for a moment and then suggested, "But even people on drugs like picnics—and their children like bouncy houses." A long moment passed in silence, and then I asked, "Did you work with any of the neighbors in planning this? There's a school down the street, a fire station, a dance studio . . . I saw those just at a quick glance as I drove in this morning. Did you talk to any of them about partnering?" "No." "Did any neighbor help in any way with the planning and execution of the event?" "No."

And there was the trouble: This event had been yet another of those sorts of affairs in which a few good church people, cloistered in the church's conference room, sought to mystically discern what the neighbors were looking for without actually talking to any of these neighbors or inviting any of them into the planning. Meanwhile, the neighbors are reading all kinds of signals coming from the church—some intentionally and some unconsciously—that are saying to them this church is a private, members-only organization, a parallel universe of sorts, where they will always be outsiders.

In this third decade of the twenty-first century, churches will rarely succeed in starting any new ministry unless they can figure out how to build a collaborative relationship with people outside the walls of *the church as it currently exists*. **A faith community emerges and grows along the contours of the leadership that you convene.** You want a church for unchurched people? Then you'd better get some until-very-recently-unchurched person to serve on the launch team. You want a church for all generations? You'd better get a good sampling of young adults on the team. You want a church of both politically blue and red hues? Do the work of cobbling that kind of community together at your leadership table. And this is true of new worship communities in general: Whatever the demographic you imagine flowing into your new community, build relationships with people in that demographic. Work with them; play with them; troubleshoot with them; and, eventually, get such people to serve as members of the team that is planning and creating your new worship community.

Your ministry will grow in the demographic direction of its launch team's circle. And until you can convene a launch team that looks like the worship community you desire to gather, you may not be ready to launch such a community.

If you are working a territory where organized religion gets a bad rap, your first community collaboration may need to be something extremely community-focused, rather than worship. Find a cause for good that resonates with local folks, and organize with them for that cause. Better yet, if someone is already organizing in the community, show up to their party. Bring volunteers. Make some friends through doing something good for society. Meet the movers and shakers who long for a better world and who also do something about it! You will learn so much and meet so many persons of interest. And among the people you meet, you will have a much larger circle from which to draw a launch team for the worship community you desire to plant.

Rodrigo Cruz is the pastor of The Nett Church[1] in Gwinnett County of Georgia, northeast of Atlanta, an organization that is, by design, a multiethnic church. Before Nett launched a weekly worship service, they began a habit of gathering to serve the community on a regular basis. For many people, a community-service event provides a much easier opportunity to invite a nonreligious friend "to church." Every fourth Sunday of the month, The Nett Church deploys its people into the community via a variety of teams for Sunday-morning service projects. And on Community Service Sunday, they are joined in these community-service projects by neighboring members of the Islamic faith. New friendships are formed in the course of this shared work. Sometimes a mission project is an easier first step into a faith community for many people. But even as The Nett Church organizes and facilitates these community-service days, still, the church counts on its members to take advantage of the opportunity to invite others whom they believe would find meaning in serving neighbors.

From new relationships emerge new possibilities.

Early in the planting of our new worship community in Northwest Florida, a highly motivated group of our church members created a Friday night Christian karaoke event at the place where we gathered on Sundays. Now, karaoke is not my cup of tea, personally—but no one was saying I needed to lead it myself or even attend. This motivated, enthusiastic group of church members could organize it better than I could, and they could invite their friends. They often had seventy-five people in attendance at the event.

Maybe your church could throw a block party or host some kind of event coinciding with Halloween. If so, bring in some other community organizations to serve on the design team. Hold the event somewhere outside the church, if you think that might help. Offer for your church to run the main stage, welcoming people and emceeing various activities and/or performances. This kind of event offers an opportunity for gently introducing to the larger community your church's vision and appreciation for fun. However, remember that a block party is not a worship gathering or a church picnic; it is a community event not primarily for the purpose of church fellowship but rather for building relationships among neighbors.

In all cases, it is a great practice to ask your launch team members and other participants in your emerging worship community to engage in projects of mission and community relationship-building to make some new friends, Then, after a few months, you can invite team members to make lists of five local people each for whom you wish to pray, and with whom you will be looking for opportunities to invite and connect. These lists can be kept on your phone or on a note card affixed to your refrigerator, the top of your desk, or your bathroom mirror. Every time you see your list, you can commit to taking one minute to pray for each person on it. This will create a sense of concern and intentionality about your relationships. And in return, the chances that you and your fellow launch team members will invite someone on that list increase.

The bottom line is this: churches emerge from a matrix of community relationships. Sometimes a church needs to develop more relationships, partnerships, and friendships within its neighborhood before its members will be comfortable inviting anyone, and before many people will be comfortable accepting such an invitation. If churches develop strong relationships in their communities and design new ministry with the people they are seeking to serve, they will usually find more people ready to accept an invitation.

10

USING COMMUNITY CONVERSATIONS TO EXPAND REACH

Kris Sledge

hurch has changed forever. The recent pandemic made obsolete many tried-and-true methods, strategies, and programs that once worked to connect new people to Jesus. As church leaders, we started asking ourselves what new methods we would need in order to share the same powerful message of Jesus' abundant life for all.

I reflected on the new methods ministry would require during this unique time. I made a commitment that our core vision to love our neighbors and connect new people to Jesus was not going to change. At The Journey Church in Harrisburg, Pennsylvania, where I serve as the lead pastor, we made the decision, similar to that of many other churches, to create an online worship experience for gathering with our worshiping community. However, I was not satisfied with *only* providing an online worship experience for my church community. We would not pause our conviction to connect new people to Jesus during months of uncertainty. We needed to pray and dream about unique ways we could expand our orbit online during this season.

In our praying and dreaming, it became clear we could not simply wait until things someday return to "normal" to live out our mission. We boldly decided we would do whatever it took to connect new people to Jesus in a digital age.

Expert Opinion, a weekly community conversation series, became our first bold decision. This conversation series became a platform for community leaders, local theologians, counselors, professionals, nonprofit leaders, and local experts to share how they understood the unique season of 2020 we were all in. We launched this Sunday-evening conversation series to create a space where our current members and our city residents could engage in relevant conversations and listen to various experts share about how they understood what was happening during the pandemic. In a season when many were questioning the relevance of church and the Christian faith, we wanted to create a space apart from Sunday mornings to host honest conversations about what was happening in our local area and in the world. We did not merely want to survive the pandemic; rather, we were convinced we could thrive and clear the way for real, life-giving conversation and community.

Our intention for these conversations went far beyond education for our church members; our foremost desire was to grow the number of people in our ministry reach. This aspiration led us to use an online platform called StreamYard that pushed our conversations to our social-media platforms. With a consistent brand, logo, and framework, we hosted conversations that were then shared around our church, our city, and the greater region. Every Wednesday, we posted the name of the speaker and the topic for the upcoming Sunday. We used Facebook's paid ads and encouraged people to invite friends, family, and community leaders who may be passionate about a particular topic to join in on that week's conversation.

Choosing which experts to interview on *Expert Opinion* proved extremely important. I selected guests to speak on *Expert Opinion* based on three criteria: their particular field of expertise, how they would challenge our church, and how well they would connect with our larger community. For example, I have interviewed the mayor of Harrisburg, a superintendent of schools, a local journalist, the police commissioner, a university president, and a local theologian because of their ability to speak to the realities of our city and current events. These guests were highly relevant to both The Journey and the Greater Harrisburg community. The real win came when the Harrisburg mayor shared the Facebook feed of *Expert Opinion* on both his personal page and the city's Facebook page. Now, the conversation would be accessible not just to those already following The Journey but to anyone connected to our city. We began to witness additional city residents who were not connected to our worship community tuning in to our weekly conversations. *Expert Opinion* became a way for anyone, regardless of faith or church background, to listen and engage through conversations about our city, the world, and faith.[1]

The default for Christian leaders is often to use social media and public conversations as a means for talking strictly about faith or simply advertising upcoming church events. This default assumes that the only relevant topics for a church to discuss are faith, Jesus, the Bible, and church programs. However, our experience with *Expert Opinion* has shown us that Christians and non-Christians alike benefit from engaging in critical conversation. In fact, *Expert Opinion* has become part of the new weekly rhythm of The Journey and our larger community. The weekly number of views for *Expert Opinion* almost doubled that of our weekly worship services, quickly expanding and widening the bandwidth of people connected to our ministry.

On Sunday evenings at 6:00 p.m., I began to go live via The Journey's Facebook and YouTube platforms. I introduced that week's expert and then spent around forty-five minutes interviewing that person with questions I had crafted and sent in advance. Before interviewing the guest, I would talk with him or her to craft a tentative framework and discussion guide for our conversation. Each live conversation had a structure and a plan, but it also remained open and flexible, based on the guests' sharing and live comments and questions. Each guest could identify beforehand any topics or questions that were off-limits. This was especially essential for guests who held public positions in our city. Throughout the conversation, I would encourage viewers to use the chat function to ask questions and to share their thoughts. People began to experience a level of community by tuning in on Sunday nights. The method was simple, and both our new friends and old friends would come back every week for learning, community, and engagement.

As I went along, I had to refine how I thought about this community series. On a merely practical level, I started off by using a complicated system to broadcast the interview on various social-media platforms. Using a simple-yet-productive platform that could handle multiple guests and stream to various other platforms was essential. As a novice interview host, I drew inspiration from several documentary series on Netflix. To coincide with my personality, these conversations needed to balance depth and relatability. I wanted anyone tuning in to be able to have both an *aha* moment and to laugh throughout the conversation. The format enabled anyone visiting our social-media platforms to have a front-row seat for the conversation. No one had to drive, order tickets online, or worry about parking to be able to hear from our mayor, local university presidents, theologians, or counselors. Instead, these conversations were highly accessible, available in people's homes or cars or wherever they access the Internet.

On a deeper level, the rise of the Black Lives Matter movement in the summer of 2020 influenced the direction of *Expert Opinion*. When our conversation series launched, we were inviting each of our guests to share, from the field of his or her expertise, thoughts relating to the global pandemic. But that summer, we found that the horrifying deaths of George Floyd, Breonna Taylor, and Ahmaud Arbery (and so many others) were influencing our conversation each week. Regardless of their profession or expertise, we benefited from hearing local leaders share how they understood and responded to the continuing deaths of Black and brown men and women in the United States. To be honest, I was humbled to hear the heart and pain of people who shared openly about these tragic deaths. All the guests (Black, Brown, and white) spoke in solidarity with our Black brothers and sisters and helped provide a framework for their own thinking and compassion in this season.

One guest, who attended and helped lead every Black Lives Matter protest and march that was held in our city and region, spoke about his experiences being a young black male in the face of opposition as he and others sought justice. He helped clarify and speak truth about these local protests, and he gave us a front-row picture of what was happening. Those who tuned in to this episode were able to ask questions, seek clarity, and understand the heart behind this movement without being physically present at a march.

The city of Harrisburg, where I pastor, is a "smaller" Pennsylvania city of about 50,000. This community size allows for local conversation to be productive and influential. People know one another well. We quickly positioned ourselves as the congregation who stood in the gap in this time. This conversation series stood in the middle and facilitated conversation between faithful Christians, local professionals, and leaders; and it activated the creativity of our viewers to faithfully respond as bearers of love and kindness in this particular time in history.

Every church leader can convene and build community to expand their reach. All you need is a willingness to create an environment and platform for someone else to speak into the life of your church and your community. Early on, I was hesitant to ask someone like our mayor to join, but if I hadn't done so, our church and the larger community would have missed out because of my own fear. Do not be afraid, because launching community conversations is not difficult. You will be surprised at how open local leaders are to sharing. You are providing them with a platform to reach a wider audience. Be clear about why you want to host these conversations and who the intended audience is. Think locally, dream of potential guests, identify specific topics for conversation, find your online voice and presence, and start inviting people to share. You will begin the slow, faithful work of building community. This holy work has the potential to greatly expand your church's relationship with your neighborhood and speaks to how the church remains relevant today.

11

GATHERING PEOPLE IN THE START-UP SEASON

Rachel Gilmore

When you have deeply invested in listening to and learning from your community, the season of gathering people can be the most energizing and exciting time in the formation of a new faith community. It's a chance for you to create spaces for all these people you have met to converse and connect with one another, so that you can fine-tune who you are as a community and better understand whom God is calling you to reach.

When it comes to gathering, start with those who would naturally want to spend time together. For me, planting a new church a few years ago in a military community during a time of high troop deployment, I approached it differently than I would have if I had been planting in midtown Manhattan. As a young mother with a baby in tow, that meant hosting and attending playdates with other moms and their young children. It meant joining with other women on their way to the Women's March in 2017. It meant hosting backyard barbecues for Navy families and joining the local meetup.com book club. For those contacts I had met who were very curious about our vision to create a safe place for "spiritual nomads," we organized small groups based on affinity so they could explore faith together. We had the "Y.A.M.s" (Young-Adult Marrieds); the "Y.U.M.s" (Young Un-Marrieds); and the "Pregs and Babes," for families who were expecting their first child or had a little one at home.

Because so many husbands were deployed and away from home as we were preparing to launch, we operated in a context of crisis and ministry opportunity, distinctive to that time and place. Similarly, think about gathering strategies during the year 2020, almost anywhere in the world: They had to be designed distinctively, depending on how the COVID-19 pandemic was affecting life in particular locales. Any gathering must, by its very design, make sense to the population you are seeking to gather, and it must feel relevant and timely for them.

As I began gathering all of these new people in different settings, I would follow the same general rules:

1. ***Make sure it's an easy gathering to invite someone to attend.*** If I had just met a person at a park or coffee shop, I would not likely invite them over for dinner in my home. That just isn't normally done, and it could make the person uncomfortable, ensuring that I would never see them again. Rather, I would ask the person from the park or coffee shop if we could meet in that same location again next week, and I'd get their phone number so I could remind them. Often, we would each bring another friend or two with similar shared interests.

2. ***Make sure it's easy for the person to back out of the gathering at the last minute.*** Although many in our society are profoundly lonely and long for connection and community, it can make us anxious to think about actually showing up, especially for the 50 percent of us who are introverts.[1] So, if someone backs out at the last minute, show them grace and invite them to a similar event in the near future with no pressure to show up. If they decline three invitations in a row without giving a reason, take them off your

contact list but keep them in your database in case they come into the orbit of your faith community again.

3. *Make sure the place where you are gathering is easy to find, especially if it's a large gathering.* If you are hosting a Fourth of July potluck meal at the local park, have signs or balloons posted clearly to show people where to find you. If you are hosting a progressive dinner at your home, make sure your house or apartment number is clearly visible and the front light is on.

4. *Make sure it's easy for those who attend to introduce themselves to one another.* There's nothing worse than having a room full of people who separate like they are at a middle-school dance. Also, be mindful of the number of people attending the gathering who are already completely onboard with this new faith community, as opposed to those who aren't familiar with it and who are there in a different context or for other reasons. In my experience, a 60:40 ratio has worked best, so when I hosted a Halloween bonfire at the beach, I tried to ensure that no more than 40 percent of those gathered were from our small-group community. This keeps someone who is disconnected from the church from feeling "ambushed" by your faith community. For some people, there is nothing more comforting in a church gathering than to bump into someone else who is new or just sticking their toe in the water too.

5. *Hold your gatherings in a variety of locations.* Think about public gathering spaces, spaces in private homes, and digital gatherings. As I started to meet and "friend" more people on Facebook, I would record Facebook Live videos or create invites that were compelling to share with others and would bring new faces into physical or digital spaces (such as Crowdcast[2] webinars, where you could be represented by an avatar and discuss issues with others in a safe and anonymous way.)

6. *Make sure you keep track of all the new contacts you are making, taking note of which events seem to resonate most with people in the community whom you feel called to reach.* If no one shows up to a particular event, which *will* happen, don't let it discourage you, and don't take it personally; think about the myriad factors (such as time, location, purpose) that might have kept people away. Always seek to learn from a failed event, and try again, incorporating changes. Trial and error is normal. Keep at it!

7. *Make sure that there is no firm "agenda" at these gatherings other than deepening relationships and beginning to cast a shared vision of what this new worship community might look like and do.* Make sure that the gathering unfolds exactly according to the way it was described in your invitation—no bait and switch! None of us wants to head off to a party and find ourselves in a worship service or vice versa. Let people know what to expect, and stick to it.

12

WHAT DO WE WANT PEOPLE TO EXPERIENCE IN WORSHIP?

Craig Gilbert and Paul Nixon

One of the most difficult questions for churches creating a new service for new people is this one: *What do we want people to experience in worship?* The discovery and collective clarification of a desired experience is a valuable step on the journey toward beginning a new worship service. It may also be a difficult question because what we know best can easily get in our way. We may discover multiple perspectives among our team members in terms of worship that has personally been meaningful to them in the past. Yet we will need to do new things—and do some old things in new ways, in order to engage a new group of people.

It is common for one or two of the launch team members to panic close to the launch date when they discover that some planned element of the service is not quite their style. For example, it could be that they have learned the worship music is going to be different than they had imagined. And then, we have to remind our teammates that we are creating this service for new people.

As we spend more and more time with churches seeking to reach people outside of their existing congregations, we are drawn to the parallels between building a service for new people in today's world and what missionaries face when they seek to bring the gospel to a new people. Missionaries meet people where they are. They don't begin with the "hard, old stuff," even if it is good, tried-and-true, and has worked for years. No, they begin by listening and by speaking in the languages, both in terms of the words and the culture, of the people they are trying to reach. They do this by connecting with certain values in the local population, as long as they do not find these to be contrary to the gospel. It is likely that the people we are seeking to reach will experience a disconnect with certain of our ideas or practices. We need to be ready to create a worship experience that will enable them to encounter God in meaningful ways.

We have all heard the expression "stepping outside the box." J. D. Payne maintains that the more important task is being able to *name* the box in which we find ourselves.[1] As we name this box, we can then decide if, how, and in what respects we wish to step out of it. We collect habits of ritual and activity in Christian worship that vary greatly from age to age and from place to place. All of us live in danger of conflating the essentials of worship with what we are in the habit of doing in worship. It is good to recognize that our worship habits and traditions put us in a box, to some degree.

So, we may wish to call a meeting of our emerging launch team to review and clarify a few things before we get too far down the road into the details of our new worship community. In this meeting, we can work through several questions. We may already have answered some of these questions by now, but we will be reminding our team of its prior discoveries and conclusions. (Think back to chapters 2, 5, and 6.) Other questions will involve work far beyond this particular meeting. But having this conversation will help our team begin imagining what this worship gathering will look like and feel like. The vision that we articulate now will be helpful to the teams that are deployed later to work very purposefully on each specific question.

Here are the questions:

1. **Whom are we seeking to reach with this new worship community?** By this point in our formational process, a few representatives of the focus population should be sitting around the design table with us as part of our team.

2. **What are the core components of experience that we wish to offer the people who share in this new gathering?** As we make up a short list of these core components, can we state why each element is essential and how it connects with our understanding of our faith, our mission, and worship itself?

3. **Is there any specific content that we imagine we will have in this new gathering that may be different from that of other services or churches?** Everything that happens in worship should be created, crafted, and presented in a way that clearly communicates the gospel, so that your focus demographic can be fully engaged. The style and instrumentation of the music we use should be carefully selected. The form of language used in the service (formal or more colloquial) should also be appropriate. What life issues and concerns of the population must we speak to? Even the order of worship needs to fit the expectations of those who will be attending or should be crafted and presented in a way that teaches and encourages participation from new participants. (We will go into greater detail on service content in chapters 22, 23, and 24. For this meeting, we won't be concerned with too much detail.)

4. **What should the spiritual and emotional tone be in this new gathering?** This may be the most important decision of all. While it should be the goal of every church to present all the various aspects of the gospel and the overarching biblical story over the course of time, every church typically has a certain "spiritual feel" to its weekly worship that remains consistent. Whether it is the majesty and formality of a worship setting that reveals to us God

on the throne or the deeply personal experience, reminding us of Jesus, our friend, cooking fish by the campfire, this spiritual atmosphere will impact the overall worship experience more than anything else.

Again, we need to think like a missionary. Considering those whom we are trying to reach with this new service, what is the best way to communicate our basic relationship with God? Some churches seek to build toward a point of spiritual decision or a fervent prayer time late in each service. Others choose to wrap up the service after the message in a very matter-of-fact manner, often because they have chosen to address tender issues of healing and spiritual decision-making in other venues. This spiritual atmosphere will also most likely influence our decorating and content choices as discussed above.

5. **What kind of relational experience do we desire for attendees?** Some churches allow people a lot of personal space during their worship services and make minimal attempts at conversation with strangers beyond a greeting at the door and possibly a passing of the peace. Perhaps they have learned that the people they serve prefer minimal encounters with strangers. Other churches' worship services are designed to help attendees meet others and make new friends. What is our goal for our worship gatherings, in terms of the experience of relationship with others?

We can't forget to discuss the way people who are in leadership (whether on stage, in the pulpit, or in the lobby) will be dressed. All attire needs to be chosen in a way that welcomes your chosen demographic while at the same time appearing age-appropriate for your leaders. From business suits to jeans and T-shirts to anything else in between, greeters, ushers, musicians, and pastors should all be in attire that says, "Come in. Be comfortable because we are!

You are welcome just the way you are." (We will go into greater detail about hospitality issues in chapter 25.)

6. **What kind of experience do we desire for people in the physical space?** All aspects of the appearance of your physical room should be considered in terms of the experience you desire for the worshiper. If you are in a new, fresh space, then you can make decisions from a blank slate. If you are repurposing a current or previously used space, then you will need to decide what should stay the same and what can be changed. Things as basic as the styles of the seating, all the way to the color of the room, are important. Even the smell of the room can make a difference. How the space looks and feels will make a lasting impression on the people who will worship there. Lighting is another key element in creating an appearance that is inviting to those who will come. From brightly lit to dim, multicolor to single color, all types of lighting will have an influence. Even just selecting basic white light comes with a choice between warm or cool and fluorescent or LED. (We go into greater detail about physical space just ahead in chapter 13.)

7. **What kind of experience do we desire for people who tune in to the digital gathering that runs parallel to the physical gathering?** Increasing numbers of people experience worship through watching their TV, phone, or computer screen. Most churches that were able to continue functioning during the COVID-19 pandemic created, by necessity, an online worship experience. In many cases, their content was never intentionally designed for the experience of an online audience. In some cases, the online experience became like watching an in-person worship service through a window: People can look in, but they remain spectators, with limited opportunities or propensity to participate. In addition, elements such as decorations, lighting, and stage placement, while

working great for "in-the-room" worship, often do little to create an atmosphere of worship for the person watching online.

Since we are creating a new worship service, we have the opportunity to design and craft all of the above areas of consideration in a way that works for both in-the-room *and* online worship. We can take the time to consider how everything we have chosen looks and engages people in both the live medium and the digital medium to create the maximum impact for our new service. (We will explore digital worship further in chapters 20 and 21.)

Let's remind our team that this new worship service is not necessarily meant to help *us* find ways to learn about, build a relationship with, and communicate with God. Our church already has a service for us; that is why we are there. Instead, this new service will provide a completely new experience that best welcomes new people not only into our community of faith but also—and more importantly—into a new relationship with God.

If you have reached this point in your reading, discussions, and planning, perhaps you have decided to move forward with the development of your new worship community and are ready to prepare for launch. It is starting to become real! The next few weeks will be exciting. In the chapters ahead, we will seek to help you take all your visioning, thoughtfulness, and preparation and turn this work into action items, detailed steps leading to the public launch of a new worship community.

13

DECIDING WHEN AND WHERE TO GATHER

Paul Nixon

Choosing a time and place to gather often proves to be a stressful fork in the road for leaders on their journey to launching a new worship community; there will rarely be a perfect answer to the question of either when or where. Each possible choice you could make will have its advantages and its challenges. You can simply hope to avoid any challenges that could be fatal to the growth of the new gathering. You may have to fudge a bit on your preferred time in order to get your preferred space or vice versa. Anytime you have a chance to try a certain space at a certain time with your chosen audience on a one-time basis before committing to it for the long term, seize that opportunity.

Considerations for the Time of Gathering

In most contexts, Sunday morning remains the time people instinctively associate with going to church. Even if they are relatively secular people, the culture has trained them to think of church as a Sunday-morning thing. For this and other reasons, Sunday-morning worship communities typically will gather more people than communities that meet at any other time of the week.

However, there are several reasons why churches may choose to launch gatherings at times other than Sunday mornings. Usually, the reason is because within their chosen audience,

- people tend to stay up (and out) late on Saturday evenings, often without children in their homes;
- people have children who engage in Sunday-morning sports activities or in weekend select-sports travel;
- people have standing golf games or tennis matches on Sunday mornings;
- people have to work on Sunday mornings;
- people are seriously into the brunch culture (keeping more people at work on Sunday mornings to make their mimosas!); and/or
- people work fierce hours all week long and feel they really need to sleep in and rest on Sunday.

Sometimes, given the population you are engaging, it is best to set the time of your gathering on Sunday afternoon or early evening, or during a weeknight. I have one friend who is toying with the idea of holding a 2:00 a.m. service on Sunday mornings for the extensive network of friends he has in the restaurant and bar industry in his community. In every case, before you launch, ask several people what time would be good for them. And test-drive the gathering at the proposed time before locking into a lease.

While there are exceptions, gatherings on Sunday evenings or other non-Sunday-morning times will tend to be smaller than those held on Sunday mornings. This could be, in part, because they are designed for populations whose members are not in the habit of church participation to begin with. Smaller gatherings are appealing for many people today, especially if there is interaction built into the design. Others enjoy the relative anonymity of larger gatherings.

In many cases, the question of when to gather for worship is interwoven with questions about the organization's overall financial sustainability. It is somewhat rare for non-Sunday-morning worship communities to become self-sustaining, unless you launch multiple gatherings—possibly including a Sunday-morning time slot. (We will say more about this in chapter 31, "Developing Financial Sustainability.")

Considerations for Where to Gather

Wherever you meet, the space should be fresh and recently renovated, if possible. Attendees' access to parking or public transportation is critical. Full and convenient accessibility for all is nonnegotiable. There must be safe access to and from your location, with outdoor security present in the form of greeters if necessary. There should be adequate space for children's ministry, reasonably close to the main gathering space. Air-conditioning is expected these days in warm weather. Lighting should be sufficiently bright and preferably dimmable. Acoustics must be workable for live music. And make sure that you can keep the space at least 30 percent full at most of your gatherings—otherwise, the space is too big.

If you need to buy chairs, think lightweight and stackable.[1] Not quite as critical, but very helpful, is having movable seating, a built-in video-projection system (that requires no setup), and a kitchen adjacent to the main room.

In terms of where to meet, let's look first at options in existing church facilities. Benefits of this choice might include the following:

- an amazing location—which, likely, you would never be able to afford if you had to buy it in today's real-estate market;
- reduced amount or no rent—and, therefore, lower overall costs;
- the ability (with permission) to renovate a space and customize it for the gathering;

- on-site storage—and, occasionally, building-staff availability for setup;
- the ability to rehearse in the space during the week;
- access to a kitchen for food preparation;
- children's facilities, ready and available in close proximity to the main gathering room—and, if the service is held simultaneously with another service in the building, the possibility of sharing a single children's ministry facility between the two; and
- where traditional sanctuary worship space is available, you may like the quaint majesty of the space as part of an ancient-modern worship design.

Challenges that may come with the use of existing church facilities might include the following:

- the lack of full accessibility or awkward accessibility;
- the inability to adjust the space as truly needed, due to building rules you find unhelpful (no drinks allowed, no touching the soundboard, no moving the chairs or furnishings from their traditional worship-service positions, and so on);
- the fact that some older church pews are uncomfortable and would have to be removed entirely for the space to be functional for a twenty-first-century public;
- too little space adjacent to the main worship space for socializing;
- decrepit, outdated restrooms;
- out-of-date children's facilities (however, sometimes a little paint and some new carpet may work wonders); and
- an aversion among your chosen audience to traditional church buildings.

So, let's think about spaces other than existing church facilities. The cost of renting space for a church that might gather 150 people can vary from $200 to $1,500 per week (for a span of two to three hours), depending upon the particular time and location. However, if you choose to use a restaurant or pub space, there may be no rent required, as long as you pick a relatively non-busy time for the establishment's business. It also may be a plus if there will be consistent food and beverage sales available to your group every time you gather (whether before, during, or after your gathering).

Don't close yourself off to the option of using non-church space before at least comparing the benefits and challenges. Possible benefits include the following:

- You are required to pay only for the actual time you are using the facilities.
- If your community grows or the space proves unworkable for other reasons, you have the option to relocate. (Sometimes we see new gatherings launch in the smallest auditorium of a cinema multiplex and then gradually "trade up" over time for larger auditoriums.)
- If the space itself is a comfortable part of people's lifestyles and weekly traffic patterns already, this can be an advantage. For example, public-school facilities are the gathering spot associated with the highest first-year attendance in new congregations in the United States.[2] This is, in part, likely related to the fact that parents of students and the children themselves are already familiar with the space.

Common challenges with the use of non-church facilities include the following:

- The costs can be high to get the facility you want, when you want it; is the crowd that you will gather here going to help pay this bill?
- It is very important to negotiate up front precisely what you need in your lease. Perhaps someone on your team has experience with this kind of negotiation. Don't hesitate to ask for what you need,

since your group will be a steady source of income for the property owners.

- On-site storage of your equipment may not be available, which will require you to secure storage facilities for use during the week and then transport your equipment to the worship-service site when you gather.
- The facilities custodian assigned to work with you may or may not be helpful.[3]
- There is seldom a guarantee that your lease will be renewed, possibly leaving your group in a pinch without a place to gather.
- Sometimes the facility has a policy requiring you to use their caterers or vendors for food and beverages. (This is seldom going to work within a church's budget.)
- You are required to develop and manage temporary signage that enables the entering public (during the hours you are gathering) to see that this is your space and that you are ready to receive them.

Try to avoid the following:

- any room where people must enter within view of those already gathered; entry should be from the rear of the room—otherwise, when people are running late, they will dread the thought of having to do a "perp walk" in front of the crowd as the band plays, and so, they will just put off attending until another week;
- a musty odor in the building; this is not just unpleasant, it could be a sign of mold—and you don't want your attendees to go anywhere near that;
- inadequate parking or access to public transportation;
- a room too small for growth (one that is already full at your first gathering) or too large (where you cannot reasonably fill 30 percent of the space). In the 2020s, it is fair to expect that many people do not wish to crowd together shoulder to shoulder, so the

room that may have accommodated 150 people in pre-pandemic times may now feel crowded with ninety—unless the median age is, say, twenty-three, in which case, they may prefer the energy of a tightly packed space; and

- high-maintenance furnishings, particularly chairs that are heavy to move or hard to clean.

If You Do Not Plan to Gather at the Same Time and Place Each Week

Many churches are looking at offering large-gathering worship that meets less than weekly, often because their most basic unit of community is a small-group network. If you plan to gather less than weekly, you will have more time to prepare for each new service, with less volunteer time required. You can have fun creatively with each service. Furthermore, a less-intense worship-production schedule could allow more time for other critical endeavors, such as serving your neighbors in direct ministry. One new worship community experimented with having pop-up worship in different times and locations, to some success. The challenge with such a lack of week-to-week predictability is this: If your most marginal constituents can't remember that this is the week for worship, or if they have lost or misplaced the information about where the gathering is to be held this week, they will unintentionally miss worship or choose to skip it. A lack of consistency and predictability about the time and location of your services will have an effect on the momentum of your new worship community.

So, if you plan to meet less than weekly or in rotating locations, you should plan to create a robust communication system—preferably one involving smartphones—to remind people when and where to meet for each new gathering.

Nothing gets more stressful in launching a new worship community than frustration about not finding a meeting place that meets your team's expectations. Again, remember this: There is no perfect place. And there is no perfect time. And, as we will underline in the pages ahead, some people will choose to connect with you digitally more often than they get dressed and travel to you.

14

THINKING THROUGH THE
TEAMS YOU WILL NEED

Craig Gilbert

While deciding who should be on your leadership team may seem like a daunting task, this may actually be one of the easiest questions to answer in the process of creating a new worship service. It is a multistep process, yet fairly simple.

As we dive into team building, here is a quick word for those of you who are looking to build a service for thirty to fifty people or who may just be getting started with your first service. If you envision a worship service with an attendance of about thirty people, then you can simplify your list of teams and combine some of the tasks to be shared among fewer people. But be mindful that even with as few as thirty attendees, a new worship community can easily burn out a small group of faithful volunteers, if teams are not organized in advance. Don't let the following brainstorming exercise intimidate or discourage you. Go through this process, and then modify it and make it your own for your worship community.

Think of the new people you are trying to reach with this new worship gathering, your chosen audience. You have prayerfully decided to focus on a specific range of people. (See chapter 5, "Focusing on a Particular Set of People," and chapter 6, "Building Bridges with the People We Seek.")

You have created opportunities to get to know them, to learn about their deepest longings, and to network them in relationship with one another. (See chapter 8, "Developing a Culture of Invitation," through chapter 11, "Gathering People in the Start-up Season.") Now, you have to pull all of these elements together to create a set of teams, filled with the individuals whom you have identified. These are the people who can accomplish the variety of tasks necessary for achieving the goal of launching a new worship service. What exactly are these teams, and what are they specifically tasked to do? I am glad you asked! Using your imagination, follow me on a journey to discover the answers.

1. Imagine the people you are trying to reach, sitting in their homes, wherever that may be. Assume that they have never heard of your church. Also, assume that they are not looking to start going to church.

2. Now, think about what it will take to
   A. inform them about your new service; and
   B. convince them to give your new service a try—to stick their toes in the water.

3. Make a list of the things you think you will need to do in order to accomplish 2A and 2B (above). (NOTE: You did some of this already, in chapter 6, "Building Bridges with the People We Seek," and chapter 8, "Developing a Culture of Invitation.")

4. The people you will need in order to accomplish the items on the list you have made is one team; I call it the Invitation and Motivation Team.

Now, let's assume this team is successful, and people decide to come try your new service. What other teams will you need?

1. Think about how the people you are designing this service for will be arriving at your gathering: Will it be by car? by public transportation? by a ride-sharing service?

2. After these people arrive, how will they know
   - A. where to park or get dropped off; and
   - B. where to enter the building?
3. Make a list of all the things you will need to address to help their arrival go as smoothly as possible *before* they actually enter the building, such as the following:
   - A. Will they be greeted by people outside?
   - B. Will there be signs to direct them where to go?
   - C. What about how the area immediately outside of the building looks?
   - D. What might increase the attendees' anticipation of discovering something good inside the doors?
4. All of the people you will need to handle the items on this list are, collectively, another team. I call this the Welcome to Our Campus/Church Team.

Okay, you are making progress; you have two teams now! What additional teams will you need? Let's assume that these first two teams have done a great job, and your hypothetical people have successfully arrived and entered the building.

1. Think about every possible place where this person may need help, such as the following:
   - A. being welcomed;
   - B. finding a restroom;
   - C. finding childcare;
   - D. finding snacks or coffee; and
   - E. finding the main worship space.
2. Remember that these are just a few examples. Make a list of all the ways in which these folks may need assistance in order to feel welcome.

3. All of the people you will need in order to accomplish the tasks on this list form another team. I call this the "Hello, How Can I Help You?" Team. (See chapter 25, "Offering World-Class Hospitality.")

You are on a roll! The new people with whom you have connected are now ready to enter the worship space. Now, you simply need to provide a worship service.

1. Make a list of all of the tasks that need to be accomplished to make your worship service happen:
   A. Who will decorate the space?
   B. Who will operate the lights (if necessary)?
   C. Who will operate the video screens (if necessary)?
   D. Who will operate the sound (if necessary)?
   E. Who will play/sing/lead the music?
   F. Who will preach (if there is a message)?
   G. Who will collect the offering (if you decide to include it)?
   H. Who will plan the entire worship service?
   I. What else will we be doing in worship, and who will make sure it happens?
2. All of the people you will need to accomplish the tasks on this list form yet another team. This is the Full Worship Team.[1] (In chapter 21, "Thinking Two Tracks: Digital and In-Person," we will discuss the smaller Worship-Design Team.)

Finally, after the service is over and the attendees have returned to wherever they began their journey, how will they know that you appreciated their joining you and you would like them to come again?

1. Make a list of all the ways you would like to communicate with the people who have tried out your new worship service.
   A. How would you like to invite them to come again?

B. How would you like to inform them about all the other things your church has to offer?

2. All of the people you will need in order to accomplish the tasks on this list make up another team. You might call it the "We Want You Back!" Team. (See chapter 26, "Onboarding New People into Community.")

Here are all the teams you have created so far:

1. communication and invitation: **the Invitation and Motivation Team**;

2. arrival and greeting (outdoors): **the Welcome to Our Campus/ Church Team**;

3. welcome and hospitality (indoors): **the "Hello, How Can I Help You?" Team**;

4. worship: **the Full Worship Team**, which includes

    a. **the Basic Worship-Design Team**;

    b. **the Tech/Offstage Team**;

    c. **the Music/Preaching/Onstage Team**; and

5. attendee follow-up and re-invitation: **the "We Want You Back!" Team**.

So, now you have between five and eight teams. Team 1 (Invitation and Motivation) and Team 5 ("We Want You Back!") are often combined. They certainly can and should work together, but you will probably reach a higher level of success if they are two separate teams, each with its own objectives, and both working in coordination with each other.

You may find that you need to create additional teams in order to reach your goals:

- Many churches have a prayer team specifically for new worship services. (See chapter 7, "Developing a Culture of Prayer.")

- You may need a team focused on coordinating childcare and youth activities. (See chapter 27, "Customizing Children's Ministry.")
- You may need a small-groups/Bible-study team, which would be focused on handling smaller gatherings for spiritual growth. (See chapter 11, "Gathering People in the Start-up Season.")

The possibilities for the different teams you might need will be very specific to the particular goals and objectives for your worship service and how you plan to achieve them. Think of every possible place where your hypothetical new people may come into contact with someone else, need help, or require information; and in all of those places, you may need to create a team to make sure those things happen.

You could be up to ten teams by now. The more people who get involved helping with a ministry related to your new worship community, the better. The most common mistake in starting a new worship community is trying to produce the weekly experience with too few people. A good target for the number of people involved on a team is one-half of your desired weekly attendance.

You may ask, "Why do you recommend the number of people directly involved in producing the service be one-half of our total attendance? Did you just pull that out of the air?" Actually, no, that percentage is initiated to intentionally work to counter the common reality of the "80-20 Rule," also known as the Pareto Principle.[2] You will most likely experience the 80-20 Rule as 20 percent of your people will account for 80 percent of the work needed to make your service successful. This is significant because while you may be able to get your service off of the ground with only 20 percent of your attendee's working this hard, eventually this workforce limitation will severely hamper your growth in myriad ways.

In my experience, a target of 50-50 for persons in active work in some aspect of the service, no matter how small, provides some advantages:

1. Your volunteers will last longer as helpful contributors. 50-50 tends to produce less burnout.

2. By increasing the amount of individuals invested in the "work of the church," you also increase the likelihood that these folks will invite others to your new service. Why? Because they are proud of the ministry they are doing, and they want to share it with others. More people working equals more potential invitations equals more growth.

3. More work investment in the service often translates into higher investments in other areas of ministry, including giving.

4. High levels of work participation can both increase "front door" visitation through sharing and decrease "back door" attrition due to inactivity, thereby significantly speeding up target gains in attendance.

Team building is the single most important strategy you can pursue to scale up the size of the full group that will gather. So, do not consider team building a chore; please look at it as your stairway to the accomplishment of your mission. It will take work, yes, but it offers the easiest and most proven way to ensure that your new worship community launches well.

Keep in mind that the minimum number of persons on a functional team is four. Any fewer, and it results not in a functional team but in a burden placed upon too few people. When you do not build your teams in an outward fashion, you invite perfectionism, control, and dysfunction among a few of your ministry leaders. And for every team, five members is more preferable than four. Yet some teams (such as the hospitality and greeting teams) can grow as your service grows, to the point where there may be dozens of members involved.

At this point, you don't have to identify the persons who will lead and build your teams. List only the teams you will need. If certain people come to mind as potential team leaders, make note of them. After two people have agreed to lead each team, it will become their job to find others to fill out their teams. In other words, building your teams can become a very tangible way to build the new worship community itself. Add the friends, family, and children of your team members, and you will reach a critical mass—a sufficient number of people to gather and discover energy in the room, week to week.

This initial formation of your teams is crucial to the future success of your new service. All the time and energy you have spent thus far making plans and decisions will mean little if you do not have an intentional path toward bringing those dreams to life. This focus on teams will enable you to organize and recruit the cadre of people you will need to help lead the way and make that happen.

15

THINKING CORRECTLY ABOUT FUNDRAISING

Gary Shockley

The image on the television screen captivated me. A man named Jerry Lewis was down on one knee, speaking eye to eye with a little boy in a wheelchair. This was the first time I had heard anything about something called *muscular dystrophy,* and, apparently, it affected a lot of children. Jerry hugged the boy; wiped away a tear trickling down his tired-looking face; turned to the camera; and then, looking directly at me, asked for my help. How could I say no? He and the Muscular Dystrophy Association (MDA) needed me to help them raise millions of dollars for wheelchairs, leg braces, and the kind of research needed to help end this horrible disease. I was eleven years old, and I became a fundraiser.

Quickly mobilizing a team comprised of my sister and two neighbor kids, I used a Creepy Crawlers thingmaker machine I had received the previous Christmas to crank out rubbery spiders and multicolored monster faces. We hastily transformed them into refrigerator magnets, lapel pins, and a kind of morose stained glass for unsuspecting windowpanes. When our inventory seemed respectable enough, we set up a card table on our street corner to display our wares. A cardboard sign taped to the table made our plea: *Help Us Help Jerry's Kids!* While two of us staffed the table, the other members of the team were busy replenishing our inventory. By the day's end, our Mason jar was packed with pocket change and crumpled bills totaling several hundred dollars. Meanwhile, in the television studio, Jerry was getting closer to breaking the previous year's *MDA Labor Day Telethon* goal and pulling out all the emotional stops. Phone calls were pouring into the telethon operators at a dizzying pace, as the board reflected the incredible generosity of corporations, local businesses, individuals, houses of worship, Scout troops, and the like.

What a thrill it was to call that phone number on the TV screen, to share what our little manufacturing and sales team had accomplished in our effort to help Jerry's Kids. Imagine the excitement of hearing our names read aloud by the spokesperson of the local affiliate! I barely slept that night, replaying the whole experience in my mind. We did something great. We helped other kids. We made Jerry Lewis cry with joy and gratitude as he sang "You'll Never Walk Alone" at the end of the telethon (which set a record at that time for televised fundraising). I would never be the same.

As I reflect on that particular year's telethon (and the dozens that took place over the years) as an adult, I am disturbed by the manipulation and lack of ethical behavior displayed by Lewis's and MDA's fundraising techniques. I would never advocate for anyone to employ these types of tactics. Even so, watching that telethon as a child was my first real introduction to fundraising, and it had a profound effect on my life.

What was your first experience raising money for—well, *anything*? Did you have a goal in mind? Maybe it was for a toy, for your sports team, for someone in need, or for a field trip. Perhaps you shoveled snow, mowed lawns, did chores for your mother, babysat your younger sibling, washed the neighbor's car, or made and sold something. You had a target, and you needed a plan that would help you hit it. What was that like for you? Think back to that experience, and reflect upon it while you read through this chapter.

I grew up in a household with fairly generous parents. They clothed, fed, and sheltered me. On birthdays and Christmases, I received lots of gifts. But one of the most important gifts I received from my parents was learning to take responsibility for funding the things I wanted beyond the boundaries of their generosity. When I got tired of the bad haircuts my father gave me, I had to earn enough money to pay for someone with proper training to do it. If I didn't like the clothing they bought me for the coming school year, guess what? I could buy my own. Which is why, at age thirteen I got my first job, washing dishes at the local diner. (I took my dad to that diner again just yesterday. I learned so much in that local dive!) I *loved* getting an envelope every week with cash inside it.

Our families of origin imprint so many things in us. Mine instilled a strong work ethic that keeps me working just as hard at the age I am now as I did when I was thirteen.

There is no such thing as "can't," only "won't."

Do it right the first time.

If it's broken, try to fix it.

If that doesn't work, then find or pay someone else to do it.

Trophies are for winners. Everyone else gets the satisfaction of trying.

I've watched my father live these maxims all my life; and now, at the age of ninety, he still does!

What are some of the maxims you learned from your family? Who was the most influential person in your life when it comes to setting a goal and going after it? What were you taught about money? about asking others for help?

I have several friends who are professional fundraisers. I recently asked one whom I particularly admire, "If you could point to one thing that keeps people from successfully raising money, what would it be?" I suspected what his answer would be from my own fundraising experiences, but I wanted him to confirm it. Here it is. It's a nasty, little four-letter word: *fear*. The fear of failing and fear of rejection: *What if I can't do it? What if I make others angry while trying?*

Some people who are genuinely fearful about this have had the experience of failing at something and/or have gotten an angry response from someone they looked up to when they asked for help. But wait a minute; that's also true for *all of us*! We've all experienced failure, and we have all disappointed or angered someone important in our lives. And we have learned to move on. We've learned new approaches to problem solving and enlisting the help of others. I firmly believe that *anyone* who has a burning passion about something can learn how to share that passion with others *and* invite their support.

I remember seeing a sign in a very low tunnel that ran from Heathrow Airport in London to our adjacent hotel. The sign read: *Mind Your Head*. I'm well over six feet tall, so I heeded the warning.

When it comes to fundraising, we have to "mind our heads." We need to tap into the strong and positive messages others have imprinted upon us and mine them for the courage and confidence we need in order to raise funds. We may also need to over-write some other messages that are holding us back.

Look back on your earliest experiences for instances of success. Success breeds confidence, and confidence leads to success. Chances are, if you successfully did something once, you could do it again. This includes asking people for money.

Sometimes fears about fundraising come from a kind of psychological projection. We project onto others our own discomfort regarding talking about money. The voice in our head says, *I can't talk to them about money because it will make them feel uncomfortable.* But who is really uncomfortable here? That voice adds to the angst: *If I ask them for money, they'll feel like I'm taking advantage of our relationship.* Was there a time when *you* felt that someone was taking advantage of your relationship with that person? Are you now projecting that negative feeling onto someone else?

"Minding our heads" means understanding the stuff that swirls around inside our brains. It means grabbing hold of that which is healthy and helpful and reinforcing it with new experiences. If you have never had a positive experience asking people to give money for something you care about, then try this: Right now, get out into the world, find someone whom you know and care about, and ask that person for twenty dollars to support a cause you are involved in. It could be something your faith community is doing to help others, a special fundraiser for a project at work, or even adding to your own money to buy flowers for a mutual friend who is going through a difficult time. Seriously, do it!

If you don't remember anything else from this chapter, remember this: *People give to people they know, trust, and care about!*

If you raised the $20 from someone you know and care about (and who knows, trusts and cares about you) then you are now catching on to how this works. That is the secret sauce for successful fund raising. Trying to raise money without this kind of relational equity is not impossible, but it is far more difficult.

Going to back to my fundraising venture for Jerry's Kids, people gave to our efforts because (1) we were kids ourselves, (2) they cared about us, (3) everyone in the neighborhood knew us and our parents, and (4) they trusted us because they knew of the annual telethon.

People Give to People They Know, Trust, and Care About

Get your thinking about money straight! Mind your head! Spend some time thinking about what you believe regarding money and/or material possessions.

Here's what I believe: I was born with nothing, and I will die with nothing. Everything in-between those two significant events in my life is mine to manage in the best way possible for the benefit of others—my family, my community, and the wider world. I want to be responsible in the way I steward my "stuff." And it is an honor to invite others to invest in the things I believe will make a positive difference in the world.

Money is not a dirty thing; *selfishness* with money is the problem. Are my material possessions simply for my own pleasure or have they been entrusted to me for some greater good?

I crowdsourced to raise money for an art project. I had to reframe my thinking about asking my friends for money. I was taught not to ask for charity but to earn everything I needed. Asking for money seemed impolite. Further, I was taught—incorrectly—that "money is the root of all evil."[1] These ideas were imprinted in my mind, so I could not gloss over them; I had to confront the ideas spinning around in my head. It helped a great deal when someone I deeply admire gave the first $500 gift of my campaign and challenged others to do the same. He used the relational equity he had with people far outside my own circles of influence to support me. This is how networking works.

When I decided to launch the campaign, I had projected that some might be offended. One friend sensed this struggle within me and challenged, "Would you hesitate to ask any of these friends to help you unload the equipment you bought for your project? Would you hesitate to ask them to pray (or cheer) for your art project?" (The answer was to both questions was "no.") "Then why," he continued, "would you hesitate to ask for their donation?" And, you know what? He was right!

Ask yourself, what is the worst thing that could happen if you asked someone for money to support something you believed in and truly felt could enhance the lives of others? Is it worth your risking the success of the project by *not* asking for support?

It's not begging if it's something you believe is worth investing in and will enhance the lives of others. You are simply inviting those you ask to become co-investors in the dream and to experience the joy in such an investment.

David Steindl-Rast has this to say about affluence:

> The word *affluence* suggests that whatever flows in never comes out. Our affluent society stays affluent by making the containers bigger when they are just about to overflow, like a fountain with its lovely veils of water spilling over. The economics of affluence demand that things that were special for us last year must now be taken for granted; so the container gets bigger, and the joy of overflowing, gratefulness, is taken away from us. But if we make the vessel smaller and smaller by reducing our needs, then the overflowing comes sooner and with it the joy of gratefulness. It's the overflow that sparkles in the sun."[2]

Human beings are, by nature, generous. When you read some of the current trends about giving in the United States, for example, you will see just how generous we are. Sadly, a great deal of this generosity is turned inward, toward selfishness. But let's "mind our heads" and get our thinking straight about fundraising: Inviting others to give to your worthwhile cause turns generosity outward again, and that is where joy begins—the joy of giving to something greater than ourselves.

16

COLLECTING EVERYTHING YOU WILL NEED

Craig Gilbert

In chapter 14. we discussed the teams you will need—real people, taking real action, reaching real accomplishments to make your worship service go. Then, in the last chapter, Gary Shockley discussed the challenge of gathering the funds necessary for the start-up. This chapter is dedicated to the *stuff* you will need—all those magical things (well, mostly mundane things, actually) that you will need to get this project off the ground and moving ever closer to reality.

Are you ready? Let's make some lists.

Let's start by understanding the difference between *the stuff you need* and *the stuff you need to buy*. The stuff you need is all the items you will need to make your service thrive. We will deal with that list right now. Your shopping list will be determined by comparing the list of the stuff you need with a list of stuff you already have or can get without buying. We will deal with that list a little later in this chapter.

HOLD UP ON THE SHOPPING! I must insert one caveat, right here, right now. I know how this goes. You have only the best intentions. You want to do what is right, but you almost can't help yourself:

You want to *shop* for stuff for this service. Not later but now. You and your team probably have already developed ideas about what you want, how nice everything will look, how cutting edge the tech will be, how comfortable the chairs, and so on. You have pored over all of the prior chapters asking you to think, pray, search, question, and then think and pray again. And now, finally, you have come to an activity for which you have great passion: buying stuff! You may have Amazon loaded up in your browser favorites, and everything you need can arrive in two days or less time. But I am asking you . . . no, I am begging you: Please wait! Read this entire chapter first. Then, if you still feel the need to shop, I won't stop you. All I can say is, "I tried"!

The Stuff You Need

This list will initially be simple for the purposes of this book. You will need to make it relevant to your specific location or room, the number of your expected attendees, your worship style(s) of choice, and so on. However, here is the basic list of the stuff you need:

1. furnishings (including seats for attendees and presenters; tables, if needed; a podium,[1] if needed; and so on)
2. lights (room lights and stage lights, if needed)
3. sound (your acoustical needs will vary based on the style of the service, the size of the room, and so on)
4. video projection (as desired)
5. hymnals, songbooks, and/or pew Bibles (as desired)
6. simple items related to basic hospitality (coffee makers, cups and plates, and so on)
7. equipment, furnishings, and curriculum needed for children
8. fresh paint and/or flooring materials (as desired, especially if any of your rooms—say, the children's zone or entrance lobby—currently look a little rough)

9. anything related to safety, sufficient to meet all local, state, and federal legal requirements and standards (You may be required to create risk-assessments for governmental or ecclesial oversight purposes. Making such assessments is a good practice, even when they aren't required.)

10. If your meeting room is too large, you may want to consider using space-dividers to help shrink it to the level of intimacy preferred.

11. anything related to online tech: What items and services do you need to make your worship service (or a comparable experience) available digitally?

Okay, that's it. Making the list of the stuff you will need is literally that simple. You may think of a few more categories to add to it as you proceed, but try not to make this harder than it is.

Next, sit down and dream about how you want the room to look and feel and how the furnishings can help with that. Hopefully, your room already has lights, but you may want something more. In older rooms, simply switching over to LED fixtures and bulbs can make a big difference without requiring an expensive overhaul of the electrical system. If there is already a sound system in the room or a soundboard available for your use, you will want to make an assessment of its usability for the service you are planning. Make a list of sound items you might want to add to make it a better fit for your worship-service needs. Video projection, if it needs to be added, comes with a lot of variables and possibilities, such as choosing between projectors and screens as opposed to televisions. You need to begin thinking about what would look good and work best in your setting. You will also need to think about cameras and recording equipment for your online presence. And you will need to have at least one computer to serve as the "brains" of the whole operation.

It is very helpful to consult with industry professionals, especially when it comes to tech. Even in selecting things such as furnishings and basic design, getting professional advice can save you a lot of time and money. A few dollars spent to get professional assistance at this juncture may save you thousands of dollars and many hours of headaches later. Sometimes sound/lighting/tech professionals and interior designers do not require you to buy anything from them. They may be available to contract as advisors only, if you prefer.

Unless your church is very different from every church I have ever worked with, there will be plenty of opinions on all these items. Sort through the opinions and the options, finalize your list, and get ready to go.

But wait—you can't go shopping quite yet; you are going to need a budget! This is not your weekly budget. This is your overall "let's get this service started" budget. You may think you know what you want on that list of stuff you just made out, but what you can actually purchase is limited by the budget your church can afford. So, right now, determine how much you have to spend on all of the stuff you need (or want) to get this service going in the right manner. Then, sit down with your list and at least gather price estimates on specific items. Then, make a new list of your items, prioritized by need, price, and budget. Got it?

Oh, but wait—I have to stop you again because this is where the train can go off the tracks at the beginning of the process. I call it the "home-improvement warehouse syndrome." It works like this. You decide you want to make some improvements around the house—a little paint, maybe some new flooring, change a light fixture here or there, and so on. So, you make a list of things you need, and you head out to the local home-improvement warehouse. You shop through your list, and then you head home, ready to go to work with all your shiny new purchases. However, after you get started on your project, you discover that you are missing a needed tool. And perhaps you also need a few more of [*whatever you are working on*]. Worse yet, you selected an item that just won't work in your situation, and you have realized that you need to make a change. Regardless, inevitably, after one or two (or *several*) return runs to the store, you discover that you have run way over the time you allotted for the project and often you've also run way, *way*, **WAY** over your projected budget!

I have seen so many churches fall into this trap when starting a new worship service. The materials list almost always begins with a *What we really need . . .* or *Wouldn't it be great if we had . . .* shopping list, the costs of which add up quickly. Often, the price tag of it all surpasses the projected budget well before everything needed is accounted for. A trained industry professional can help you prioritize the items on your list. Very often, there is an item that a team member thinks should be at the top of the list, when really, if you talked to a professional, you'd discover it should be toward the bottom.

So, what is another way to approach this project that could save you time and, most of all, money? I call it "The MacGyver Approach."

The MacGyver Approach

Back in the late 1980s (and then in a reboot beginning in 2016), there was an action-adventure television series called *MacGyver*. The protagonist, Angus "Mac" MacGyver, was brilliant guy who led every episode solving complex problems, fighting crime, and so on by using his wits, whatever items he could find around him, his Swiss Army knife, and a roll of duct tape. Put all these things together, and it seemed as if there were literally *nothing* this guy couldn't make or build to solve any problem. We are going to use this show as inspiration to develop a step-by-step method for gathering materials *before* you start shopping for new stuff, allowing your budget to stretch as far as it can.

Items Already In-Hand

The first thing you need to do is what MacGyver does when he needs to solve a problem: Make a comprehensive assessment of all of the stuff you already have. Go through the room you have selected and determine what is already there, ready to use. Then, go through every room, closet, storage space, and so on in your church to see what other things may be lurking around that can be pressed back into service. Remember, a MacGyver approach succeeds because MacGyver finds new uses for old, usually discarded items. By the way, many people from the Millennial Generation have proven themselves highly adept at this skill. Take a look at social media and e-commerce sites such as Pinterest and Etsy, for example, for all kinds of repurposing ideas. Even better, find someone on your team who is good at repurposing and put that person to work. Better still, find people who are not yet on your team, and share with them how you believe they have what it takes in this regard!

Now, go to your teams and ask them to work their connections to see what items you can find for little or no money. There may be things in their homes you can use. I know that after years of playing in bands, I have enough sound equipment, cables, and instruments just sitting around gathering dust to equip a small- to medium-sized room. You can also check with other churches in your area. Don't be afraid to ask another church's staff about items they may have stashed away and are no longer using, things you might be able to use or repurpose; you may find just what you need, and they may be glad to get rid of stuff they aren't using and free up their limited storage capacity. (I have set up many solid, great-working sound systems this way, saving thousands of start-up dollars.) Department stores in your community that are closing may be selling their shelving, adjustable cabinetry, or other fixtures as they are going out of business. You might get an item that would have cost hundreds or even thousands new for next to nothing, one that could be used in your church's lobby, in the children's area, or for storage.

Remember, you can always upgrade later if needed. Purchasing certain things you really want for the worship service could be delayed until you have a good determination of whether or not your new worship community is going to work. Or it may be that once you have lived into the new worship service for six months, you will discover that you are not using one particular tool you purchased nearly as much as you had expected, and you really need an upgrade in another area, so you may decide to sell that underused item in order to create funds for the thing you need more. If you have equipment that will work for now, there is nothing wrong with delaying bigger-ticket items until after your new community is up and running.

Make your list, gather those items, and get ready—possibly—to be amazed.

Now, you can sit down with the two lists you have made—the list of stuff you need/want and the list of things you have. Then, you can apply the MacGyver Approach.

Wits

MacGyver's primary tool was his knowledge of seemingly everything. In addition to your own abilities, you have two ways to take advantage of wits: finding knowledgeable people and using the Internet. Find people who are actually knowledgeable in the various areas covered on your shopping list. Inquire whether they will donate their time to advise you on this project. Even if you have to pay them for their time, the investment may save you hundreds, even thousands, of dollars in the end. Use these people's expertise and the Internet to assess the items you have previously collected, and determine how many of them can be repurposed for use in your new worship service. Remember, the knowledgeable people you consult may be able to see potential uses that you cannot.

Swiss Army Knife

Next, begin working with those usable items you have identified. Start to envision all of the different ways they could be used. I have seen tables converted into pulpits and a collection of nonmatching chairs arranged in an eclectic way that surprisingly became warm, inviting, and even homey. As I mentioned, I have built sound and projection systems out of "retired" parts, often needing to supplement with only a few newer items to make the system ready for use. Be creative, imaginative, and prayerful, and don't be afraid to try different things. After all, if a repurposed item ends up not working out, you haven't lost anything, and the possibility of gaining something wonderful—and possibly *free*—is worth the effort.

Duct Tape

Somehow, in MacGyver's world, there doesn't seem to be anything that can't be fixed using just duct tape (and, perhaps, some bailing wire). I refer to duct tape in this context as that magical "something" that takes an item precariously close to failing and makes it work. In my experience, every team has a member or two who have a "duct-tape-type brain" that is perfectly suited to solving all of those final "If only we could get this to work," problems. Find those persons, treasure them, and let them work their magic.

This entire process is another great way to get your new worship community involved. If the people you are inviting have a chance to invest, work, and provide direct input into the creation of their worship space together, they will be plugged in before you even get started! Until you ask, you'll never know what new skills and talents you will find among your new worshipers.

Okay—now, you have made your list of the stuff you need. You have determined your budget. You have taken an inventory of the items you already possess and have compared the list of items you need with the list of things you already have. You have applied the MacGyver Approach, been incredibly creative, and saved money in every area possible.

Now—finally—you can go shopping!

17

ASSEMBLING YOUR
WORSHIP-DESIGN TEAM

Craig Gilbert

With your goals and objectives for the new worship service now clearly set, you are ready to begin assembling the core worship-design team that will lead this work. It is possible that the team members who created the vision for the new service may be the best choice for also planning and building it; by this point, they certainly are some of the most informed people when it comes to the parts of the vision that will be used to drive the new design. Yet if there are some key people who were not selected to be participants in the visioning conversations, then you will want to select them for the planning portion of this endeavor. Also, you may have some people who brought great value to the visioning but who are not as gifted in bringing that vision to life in a form that can be produced on a weekly basis.

So, whom will you need? We have a few suggestions. Although their exact job titles may differ from those in your context, read the descriptions here and match them to your own people as closely as possible.

The Pastor(s)

While this may seem like an easy thing to understand, there are several realities in churches of different sizes when it comes to choosing which pastor(s) will be a part of the launch team.

The Preaching Pastor

In some churches, the pastor who will be preaching at the new service is not the lead pastor for the larger church. It is imperative that the pastor who will be preaching most of the time is on the launch team, even if it is remotely, from another location. This pastor should be a contributor to the overall design of the service. There is no reason to spend time building and launching a service where the preaching pastor is not comfortable with the service they will be leading.

The Lead Pastor

If the preaching pastor for the service is an associate or campus pastor, the pastor who is responsible for the overall vision of the entire church may want to be on the launch team as well, at least intermittently. If not, they will most certainly need to be in the loop regarding the worship-design team's work to be sure the implementation of the vision continues to fit the overall vision of the church. It is often easier if the lead pastor is on the team from the beginning and observing the process from its origins. This allows the lead pastor to better understand the conclusions that are drawn with the final design. However, it should be noted that the lead pastor must also understand that the preaching pastor for this service may, at times, have more to say about the final design than the lead pastor.

In Paul Nixon's book *Multi: The Chemistry of Church Diversity*, there is a section dealing with the critical and collaborative relationship between pastors as related to a new worship community. Too many new faith communities are sabotaged when there is a lack of alignment among the pastors and/or lack of attention given to the unique context of each worship community.

The Music Leader

Regardless of the eventual style of the worship service, it is certainly important that the person who will choose, develop, and lead the music is on the worship-design team. This is the person who best understands the resources currently available in the church, the strengths and weaknesses of the current music program, and what will be needed if musical choices are made that will require the inclusion of players, singers, sound and tech, lighting, and anything else outside of those parameters.

If you are hiring a new person to oversee the music in this new service, there are some very serious considerations that must be taken into account. I will go into greater detail about the music leader—including when and how to hire and more—in chapter 23, "Selecting Music and Musicians."

Visuals

These days, almost all new worship services include some sort of projected visual elements. This is often the case even in very traditional worship formats. Around the world, we see screens displayed in every kind of facility, even ancient cathedrals. It can be very helpful for the person who will be bringing your worship services to life each week using video screens to be part of the design process. People with expertise in this area know what works now and what might be done in the future, and they often have forward-looking perspectives: "You know what would be great in our service . . . ?"

The people who will bring the best skills in terms of visuals and other technical leadership often are younger and have been less active in past church participation than the average person in your church. As such, they often serve to broaden the life perspective of the worship-planning team. You may have to work harder to convince younger, more experienced, and/or more creative people to come on board. But don't just settle; do the work. Buy them coffee, listen to their stories, hear their ideas, and prove to them that they not only will be heard but also will be given room to create. The only thing worse than not going after the talent you need is recruiting that talent and then restricting them to working within a tiny box of predetermined ideas of what is right and good. Remember, you are building this new worship service to get *out* of a box. People with skill and creativity in the area of visual arts are just the types of talented people who can lead you there.

A Facility Coordinator/Decorator

This is someone who makes sure the building is set up properly each week. While he or she may or may not bring a high level of creativity to the process, this person will provide practical insight into what is possible in the selected space. The facility coordinator or facility decorator does not have to be a member of the worship design team, as long as someone on the team is responsible for communicating with them after every meeting. However, in my experience, it can be very helpful if the facility coordinator/decorator is part of the worship design discussions from the beginning. As this person listens to the plans that are emerging, they are thinking about the logistics involved from start to finish. This is a person who, you will find, may solve problems before you even know you have them.

The Online Coordinator

Depending on how you will be approaching your online presence, your worship design needs the input of the person who will be responsible for making that worship service available to people who are not in the room. The online coordinator should be your eyes and ears for integrating that perspective into your worship designs. In some cases, he or she may captain an entirely different team that takes the big ideas of the in-person worship service and creates something that is more appropriate and relatable for the community gathered via the web—perhaps an online experience that is shorter in duration than the main service, say, thirty minutes or so. While your team may be accustomed to building worship services that work for people in the building, the online coordinator should be constantly thinking about how the service works for and engages those who attend from other locations and at other times. (For more about the role of the online coordinator, see chapter 20, "Connecting Well in a Digital World," and chapter 21, "Thinking Two Tracks: Digital and In-Person.")

Connecting the Teams

Finally, look back at all the teams you envisioned in chapter 14, "Thinking Through the Teams You Will Need." At least one person on your worship-design team will need to be the lead contact person for the leaders of each of the other critical teams, for the purpose of communicating about the overall worship service. It is also extremely helpful if at least once every quarter, you invite all the various team leaders together for a rundown and assessment of progress that includes the point of view of every point of contact in the service. These large meetings provide wonderful opportunities for people to see the interconnectedness of their efforts. It is too easy to become siloed from one another, failing to realize how each team depends upon the success of all the others for the success of your new worship service.

Now that you have the worship-design team built, all you need to do is learn how to work together. And as you will soon see, we wrote chapter 19, "Running Good Meetings," precisely for that purpose.

18

NURTURING
MULTIETHNICITY

Tyler Sit

Many ministry leaders are interested in building multiethnic teams, and for good reason. Projections suggest that white people will be in the minority for the first time in US history by the year 2045.[1] This means that forward-looking white church planters and pastors have new motivation to create racially diverse teams, for the sake of keeping the church effective in the future.

As a church planter of a multiethnic church that is made up of 90 percent millennials and Gen-Z—New City Church in Minneapolis, Minnesota (grownewcity.church)—I have witnessed a sea change in church-planting circles, particularly after the racist murder in our city of George Floyd, which happened only a short walk from where we worship. Five years ago, I frequently heard people refer to New City Church as a niche ministry that was good in terms of "mission" but not the future of the church overall. Now, pastors call on me regularly to consult with them on how to make the future of the church more racially diverse.

As a preface to what I have to share, it's worth noting that this is advice I give to white church planters or white churches who want to diversify, though many of these principles also hold true for racially homogenous communities of color (such as, for example, a Korean ministry).

I readily note that I am not an expert but rather a practitioner: I pass along what I see working, but I make no claims to being a preeminent authority on this subject matter. My perspective is informed by my identity as an Asian American and an openly gay man. Much of my formation has sprung from mentorship and guidance in both of those communities. My earliest formation in these conversations, though, came from my childhood home. I am the son of a first-generation immigrant from Hong Kong and a third-generation immigrant from Germany. (I tell people I am half Chinese and half white.) I have seen firsthand that multiethnic community is both possible and wonderful! My parents showed me that other cultures are not threatening but insightful. They taught me that the discomfort required to cross cultural divides is more than manageable with the love God gives us. They also showed me that multiethnic community requires risk and how if you're not doing it for the right reasons, you will get twisted into all sorts of knots. With the preparation I received from my parents, I have continued on to live on four different continents, learn from various cross-cultural community builders, and plant a multiethnic church. After all of this, I eagerly affirm that the counterintuitive, life-giving work of a multiethnic ministry is a pursuit that is indeed worth fighting for.

Three Principles to Consider *Before* Constructing a Multiethnic Team

Principle 1: Your inner work will always show in your teamwork.

The reason why I am more hopeful about the church than I am about the nonprofits, businesses, and social movements I have been a part of is because the church intentionally creates space for inner work. It's common for us to use language around prayer, discernment, calling, vulnerable conversations, and even repentance; all of these are important practices that reflect an understanding of humans as being more than a composite of actions. As the pithy saying goes, "We are human *beings*, not human *doings*," and we remember that best when we attend to spiritual practices in community.

Church planters come under a lot of pressure to produce output: generating contacts, organizing events, leading teams, slamming through sermon prep . . . There is so much to do—for any ministry but *certainly* for start-ups—and it is easy to lose track of your soul in the process.

And in such a pressure cooker, a lack of inner work on the leader's part will always show through. This is true for the leader of any ministry team, and it is *especially* true for leaders of a multiethnic team.

The reason for this is because multiethnic teams require discomfort. Any time people from two different cultural understandings come together, it will be at least *a little* uncomfortable. I name this because at some point, the going will get difficult. And the cultural distance present in the space will magnify that difficulty. It is common for leaders who do not expect discomfort to want to give up once the discomfort comes, because they think they are doing something wrong. Yet this is a key misunderstanding. The discomfort does not mean something is wrong; rather, it means that something is *emerging*. But when people experience discomfort in an *unintentional* way (in other words, not consciously moving through it with the larger picture in mind), it can bring out bad habits. And bad habits mixed with cultural misunderstanding are enough to sink any ministry.

However, when we have developed good habits with our spiritual practices, we are able to tend to our discomfort with the three gifts named in 1 Corinthians 13:13, namely,

- *faith* ("I believe this will be worth it in the end");
- *hope* ("I know that it is possible to learn and change to be better"); and

- *love* ("I believe that God's love can see us through").

In addition to core practices such as praying, reading scripture, and sharing in community, it is also important for the whole team to see holistic health as part of its spiritual work. This can include therapy, working out, managing your budget, investing in relationships, having hobbies, and more. Cross-cultural relationships have their best chance when everyone shows up with their best.

ACTION STEPS

- Assemble a circle of support and accountability around yourselves that includes discipleship, mental health, physical health, and all the other interwoven dimensions of your well-being. This support community should extend beyond a person's ministry team or church circle.
- Commit as a ministry team to being unafraid of discomfort, and increase your capacity to navigate conflict through disciplines such as nonviolent communication, the Intercultural Development Inventory (IDI)[2], and more.

Principle 2: Work so that your commitment matches your intentions.

There are two key questions for people building multiethnic teams to keep in mind:

1. Why do I actually want to start a multiethnic team?
2. What would I sacrifice to make it happen?

When the depth of the *why* for starting multiethnic teams matches the height of the *how* for what you are willing to sacrifice, then you're setting yourself up for success. Often, though, people have aspirational, even noble, responses to the first question; but they haven't been honest with themselves on the second. This dissonance sets people up for hurt, particularly people of color. The following are some common instances where I see that happening:

People may say . . .	. . . but without real commitment, they're saying:
"We want good representation onstage."	"We like diverse optics, but we're not willing to work to change our community so that people of color will like coming here, even when they're not on the stage."
[We want to start a multiethnic team] "Because [*Black, immigrant, undocumented, and so on*] people are oppressed."	"We are aware that racist things happen 'out there,' but we're not willing to interrogate how we, ourselves, participate in racism."
[We want to start a multiethnic team] "Because we want to be a church that doesn't see color."	"We believe that God created all people as children of God, but we are unwilling to meaningfully acknowledge how some children of God benefit from racism and some children of God are brutalized by it."

ACTION STEPS

- Individually or as a team (if you are already assembling people), write out your answers to the two questions above. Compare these conversations to your budget, your decision-making structure, and the leadership of your ministry. Do the resources and power reflect your commitment to building a multiethnic ministry?

Principle 3: Make your ministry a place that addresses racism head-on.

If you don't believe that racism is real, don't build a multiethnic team. Because whether or not you believe racism is real, the social disparities are real, and creating multiethnic teams without acknowledging that is a form of denying reality. Study after study demonstrates that your skin color deeply influences the quality of healthcare you receive, your likeliness to be hired for a job, the quality of your public education, and more. Racism affects every aspect of life. Pretending that racism does not exist is to pretend that people of color do not exist. This is maddening.

Having a Black person on your team does not make your team antiracist. Opposing systems of domination and power, learning the history of race in America from the perspective of people of color, and actively pressing for change makes you antiracist.

But let me be clear: This was never about perfectionism. No leader, team, or community can oppose something as insidious as racism and not make mistakes. Therefore, the posture we seek is one of humility, not humiliation. People of color don't want you walking on eggshells whenever you talk about race, but we also want you to move if you find out that you're accidentally standing on our neck.

And let me say this to white leaders: This does not simply apply to you as an individual. If you see another white person saying or doing something problematic, you have an opportunity to intervene, so that a person of color does not have to educate yet another white person about their own oppression. All of this, when built upon the compassionate foundation of spiritual practices, can counterintuitively draw communities closer together—after all, it is not just the virtue of a community that creates belonging but the knowledge that we will be lovingly corrected if we mess up.

ACTION STEPS

- Engage resources (Bible studies, books,[3] articles, curriculum, denominational resources, and so on) on antiracism, and discern how God is calling your ministry to oppose racism. Any people of color who educate on this topic should be compensated and/or in deep relationship with your church.
- Make a list. Beyond words, what actions communicate that your team is moving toward antiracism?

I enthusiastically support ministries with multiethnic leadership. Diverse people collaborating together create incredible community, adaptive solutions to tough problems, and a story that shows the world that another type of world is possible through the love of God. Multiethnic community is amazing; however, it is also the sweet fruit of deep commitment and great love. With the commitment to the three principles outlined above, I pray that you and your team will go and change the world in beautiful ways!

19

RUNNING GOOD MEETINGS

Craig Gilbert and Paul Nixon

Most good meetings around creative activities are characterized by a free and healthy exchange of ideas rather than a top-down directive-only model. So, in an attempt to model what a good meeting on the subject of running a good meeting might look like, here is a conversation between our authors.

Paul: Craig, you and I have both spent what seems like years of our lives in church-related meetings, both leading them and attending them. Sometimes they are life-draining, and at other times, they feel so energizing and productive. You've developed strong opinions across the years on how to run a good meeting. What is required for a good meeting, in your experience?

Craig: For our purposes, I believe there are four keys on which to build for establishing, running, and succeeding in worship-team meetings: ground rules, agenda, roles, and prayer.

Paul: Before you unpack those, you had an experience about fifteen years ago that revolutionized how you approach a meeting. What can you tell us about that?

Craig: I began participating in—and, eventually, leading—worship-planning meetings in 1995. Initially, I found the meetings exciting, but I soon learned that what came out of those meetings was rarely executed as planned; often seemed fragmented at best; and, sometimes, even failed miserably. Even when I finally was put in charge of the meetings, no matter how hard I tried, I was discouraged by how often the resulting worship service made me wonder if we had even met and planned at all! Then, in 2006, something happened to me that changed my meetings forever.

I came to a point in my life where I felt like I needed to give something back to the city where I lived. I was convinced by friends to run for mayor, and I won the election. Now, all of a sudden, I was running some of the biggest meetings of my life!

Paul: I'll bet you have stories! And we think church meetings are challenging. It must have been harder to run a city meeting, given that you were dealing with an even wider diversity of opinions and concerns than most churches experience.

Craig: Yes and no. Yes, people were sometimes on different pages from one another, with radically competing visions and agendas for the city. But thankfully, these meetings were governed by a set of procedures and rules mandated by my state. This was such a gift: ground rules! Learning these rules, then planning and running the city council meetings by those rules, provided a clarity and focus to my meetings that I carry with me today. Furthermore, learning how to diffuse an irate taxpayer in an open, public forum, with cameras on all the time, is a crucible that molds some serious meeting skills! My time spent as mayor changed everything.

Paul: A lot of church leaders cringe when we start talking about rules to order a meeting, but they really can be a gift, can't they? Sometimes a meeting without clear rules can devolve into a meandering monologue by the group leader, the staff person, or the chair. And that can be painful, even when we agree with most of what is said.

Craig: Absolutely. You hopefully have some talented people around the table. A big part of the meeting is to engage them, not to anesthetize them. I don't believe you need a documented set of rules to govern your meeting. But for a meeting to be successful, at least the leader of the meeting needs to have a basic understanding of how to do the following:

- move through an agenda;
- hear input in an effective manner;
- work through difficult portions of discussions; and
- make sure that the meeting is fair to all concerned.

Now, I have been in plenty of meetings where none of this happens. But I also know that if you followed the chapters in this book and built the team we are coaching you to build, then, when you sit down to meet, you are looking at an amazing group of people who all have something important to contribute. Don't you want them to be able to make a difference in this new ministry you are building? Then, asking the team to be guided by an effective set of rules will go a long way toward that success.

Paul: Do you use *Robert's Rules of Order*?

Craig: Sort of. Learning Robert's Rules gave me an understanding of how to lead a meeting in a way that honors everyone's input but still enables the forming of what one hopes will be consensus. However, no matter what, the result will be some sort of resolution that is ready for action. Whatever method a leader uses as inspiration, whether a formal order, prior experience, or just an inviting personality, developing a method for leading a meeting, imbued with a healthy dose of Christian love and understanding, will allow the meeting to produce results. And this works regardless of the topic, from finances to facilities to ultra-creative artistic discussions. All meetings become more productive with a clear set of expectations that govern how information and ideas are to be shared and heard by everyone present. The result is happier and more-productive people, who leave feeling like they made a difference—which, in turn, usually makes them more productive as well.

Paul: I always get nervous about attending a meeting without an agenda; I feel like we are about to waste our time. And I am sometimes guilty of calling quick meetings without a formal agenda. But when this occurs, the meeting had best be focused on a very singular matter.

Craig: The agenda doesn't have to be published. It could just be a list of items on a white board. The point is that an agenda builds a good flow to the meeting. This produces consistency in productivity. I have found, for instance, that worship services that suffer from poor flow are often planned in a meeting that also has poor flow. One begets the other. When your team arrives for a meeting and there is a productive pattern to the flow, then you will find that productivity is the result. After years of trying a variety of agenda arrangements, I finally realized that if we were going to discuss and plan worship, then perhaps my worship flow could be my guide for my agenda. That way, we actually let God's plan for worship guide our own path for planning worship!

Paul: As I think about this, I suspect that what you are calling "good flow" is experienced by a lot of us in the meeting as simply energy or momentum. We feel like things are going somewhere, hopefully toward resolving a question or framing a new endeavor. But behind that good momentum, we usually find a good road map, otherwise known as an agenda. And it's funny, your connection between meetings and worship services: Services with energy have a road map—often printed and placed in our hands, but almost always in the hands of those who are guiding us! So, a clear road map can energize us, but a lot of agendas are so perfunctory and deadening; they promise to lead nowhere. So, not just any agenda will do.

Craig: Agreed. The agenda is just a road map that is created to help us best arrive at the goals we have for the meeting. But if we have no clear goals—if we are just meeting for the sake of meeting—it will be deadening. We have all sat through meetings where we left wondering why that meeting was necessary. Sometimes this is the result of poor meeting management; but often, it is because the team is meeting just because it is "time for a meeting." The team leader needs to come into every meeting with clear goals and/or objectives to be accomplished in the meeting. Without these, I can assure you, the team members are left thinking, *Why are we meeting?*

Paul: You mentioned prayer as a basic component of a good church meeting. I have heard it said that if we are on God's team, we should talk to God when we are in a huddle about God's work. Seems logical.

Craig: Prayer should be first on your agenda, last on your agenda, and anywhere else it is needed in your meeting. I have stopped meetings that were beginning to get contentious and nonproductive for time in prayer. It is amazing how a minute or two of silent prayer will calm heated emotions and return the meeting to a productive path. Prayer should also happen prior to coming to the meeting. I often remind my team members that I expect (read: *require*) them to spend time in prayer prior to every meeting. I expect them to ask God to guide their personal thoughts, to lead their speech, and to open their ears to hear all who attend and contribute. I also ask (read: *strongly encourage*) my team members to reserve time immediately following a meeting to ask God to help what has been decided and what is left to be considered sink into their daily walk, so that they can be the leaders they have been called to be and have agreed to be.

I have sat through way too many meetings that were ostensibly about God, God's plan for worship, God's plan for the life of the church—including decisions about the best way we could effect those plans—*yet God was never consulted during the meeting.* Maybe at the end of the meeting, we would ask God to bless what we had planned. But sometimes we didn't even take the time to do that.

Paul: I sometimes find there to be a need for centering prayer in a meeting, rather than a wordy prayer that leaves little space for the Spirit to work in us—quietness for a minute or two, and then a spoken prayer that bridges us from the quiet into the work we have come to do.

Craig: Paul, what, if anything would you add to my four keys for establishing, running, and succeeding in worship-team meetings?

Paul: I might add just one thing and ask one question. In my work with long meetings—such as team retreats—I have discovered a formula for a fruitful gathering. It goes like this. In the first third of your time, find a way to allow each person to sparkle, somehow. For some people, it could be that they get to show us how well they did with the financial report; for others, they may have selected a poem to read before the prayer time; while for others, maybe they played an instrument and shared some music with us. For some, maybe they told a joke. For others still, perhaps they made something to eat. I used to have a church member named Lillian who made pecan pralines that were as good as those you can find in any Mexican restaurant. I invited her to make those sugary snacks several times each year. The point of all this is that I want as many people as possible to shine, so that others say, "Wow, this is an amazing group; I am lucky to get to come out to this meeting tonight and hang with such talent!" At the same time, I want each person to feel as if he or she has been seen and appreciated by the larger group, by as many as possible. This is hard to accomplish in a short meeting, so you may have to spread it out, so that it takes two meetings to work everyone's best moment in. I have learned that if people feel appreciated and also feel a big wow about the team they are with during the first third of their time together, they will work like Clydesdale horses in the second third of the meeting; and I've also observed, then, that any actions that are envisioned in the final third of the meeting, they will actually follow up on and do!

Craig: You have just hit upon one of my keys to a great meeting: Start with the positives! I always start with *thank you*'s for work well done following through on the goals of our last meeting. We take turns around the table and share celebrations of where the things we have decided and enacted have borne fruit.

There is never any trouble finding negatives, so I want to make sure that we spend quality time reminding ourselves that we are more than our shortcomings. When we start a meeting that way, I find that we almost always take the difficult criticisms with a much healthier perspective.

Paul: Here's a question: Have you learned anything about the makings of a good online meeting that is worth adding here?

Craig: Actually, online meetings can be a conundrum. While they can be very effective, they can also be tedious and stifling to creativity. The burden for an effective online meeting really falls on the leader. Around a table, physically together as a team, there is usually a natural, kinetic energy that can drive discussion and creativity. Unfortunately, that energy rarely translates online. The leader typically needs to be more intentional about calling people by name and encouraging their participation. It is much easier for members of the team to hide and not contribute when you are using this format. Time management may also be a factor. This can be better facilitated when the meeting is set up in such a way that the leader can control all the participants' microphones; muting and unmuting as needed allows the leader both to speed up participation and limit unwanted interruptions.

Regardless of the place and time and whether your meeting is physical or digital, if a meeting is planned well and conducted as planned, you will find over time that your team will operate at the highest efficiency possible. Your goals give you a destination and purpose for your meeting. Your agenda will provide the road map to get you there. The rules, like traffic laws, will make sure you are able to follow the agenda to your goals in an efficient manner with few or no injuries or casualties. Of course, all of this will be covered in prayer, so that God will be glorified in your work together.

20

CONNECTING WELL IN A DIGITAL WORLD

Derek Jacobs

There are many different settings churches have used over the years to connect with people, including venues such as church buildings, bars, coffee houses, movie theaters, local schools, and social media. Each of these has provided people with relevant opportunities to engage and connect with one another.

But I wonder if we don't still spend most of our time, energy, and resources trying to connect with people through the use of physical spaces rather than through social media and the digital domain? In recent years, it seems that social media has become the way most people use to connect with one another and build relationships. Everywhere you go, people are on their smartphones, tablets, and laptops, engaging with one another. There are social-media experts everywhere. And it is not just young people who are connecting with one another this way, it's people of all ages.

At the church I pastor in Dallas, Texas, my oldest member is ninety-five-years-old, and she has a Facebook page. Even before the COVID-19 pandemic, when she couldn't come to church, she regularly watched our worship services on Facebook. Now, in the wake of 2020, more and more people are connecting and attending worship using social media than ever before. The pandemic forced us into social-distancing and sheltering in-place for months, closing the doors of our church buildings. This left many churches scrambling, trying to figure out how to continue connecting both with their existing congregations and with new people. How many churches were prepared for these kinds of changes? Was the church you serve prepared for the pandemic by having a social-media broadcast ready to go to continue connecting with people and inviting people to take part in worship? Even if the church you serve is not active on social media, we all need to realize that our people are immersed in social media every day—and that is the case now, more than ever before.

In Matthew 28:19-20, Jesus says, "Go therefore and make disciples of all nations, baptizing them in the name of the Father and of the Son and of the Holy Spirit, and teaching them to obey everything that I have commanded you. And remember, I am with you always, to the end of the age." In the 2020s and beyond, Jesus' Great Commission to us to go where the people are and spread God's love would surely seem to include the use of social media, which can allow us to continue connecting with people in our congregation, as well as with people who will never set foot in our church buildings.

So, how do you connect well and effectively? Consider these suggestions for your social-media strategy.

- Decide on a central social-media platform you want to use. Make sure that this platform is accessible by your audience and that people can tune in and connect with you from anywhere in the world. Some of the most-popular platforms that many churches use include Facebook, Twitter, and Instagram. In my experience, I have found that it is good to have *one main platform* and use it to push out most of your communications. This keeps things simple, both for your leadership team and for the people who are looking to connect with you. Remember, the purpose is not to do it all; instead, the purpose is to *do it well*.

- On the production end of things, choose a streaming device with a minimum resolution of 1080p (Full HD). When streaming worship, for example, you want your viewers to come back and to invite others to connect. Poor-quality video will only frustrate viewers and move them to search for another church that is providing excellence. It also gives people a bird's-eye view into the type of ministry you provide.
- Use a tripod for your streaming device. Based on my experience, I would not consider the use of a selfie stick to be effective when streaming. Holding the device will produce a shaky broadcast. Viewers want to have a clear and steady experience.
- Make sure the broadcast sound quality is good. Test it often. It is important that the sound not be muffled or too low. Viewers and listeners need to be able to hear what we are communicating clearly.
- Check to make sure the network you are using is strong enough for streaming and recording. A weak network can cause your live broadcast to buffer and pause during streaming. This will frustrate viewers to leave the broadcast. (If you suffer from unpredictable Wi-Fi, you can hardwire directly into the Internet for a faster, more dependable connection. Any number of IT experts in your church and community will be happy to show you how to do this.)
- When streaming your worship service, make sure to go live at least five minutes before your scheduled service time. I learned this the hard way. We were preparing for worship, and all our equipment had checked out just fine. But when we went live at our scheduled time, our steaming device jumped off our Wi-Fi connection. We had to scramble to fix the problem and ended up going live five minutes late. Now, a delay of five minutes might not sound like a long time, but people expect us to start on time. Going live early allows us to work out any unforeseen problems.
- Make sure the background of what you are streaming is clean and clear of unnecessary objects. I suggest enlisting a sign company

and creating a nice backdrop. The backdrop can be branded with your logo and website information. This is practically free advertising and marketing. It gives people, especially new people, a way to find out more about your ministry and to support it financially.

- Two or three days before your streaming event, make sure to invite your viewers to attend by using your social-media platform. This can be done by posting, sharing, tagging, liking, promoting, and encouraging your people to host watch parties. I also think it is very helpful to post and comment often and to make sure the content is relevant. We do not want to be a ghost on our social-media platform.

- Be authentic to who you are as a ministry. By nature, I am a fierce competitor, and I like to have fun. Therefore, we post content that challenges people and makes people laugh. Consider providing opportunities for interaction. "Boring" will not cut it online— people will quickly move on to other online ministries or activities.

- Identify one or more persons in your congregation who can lead your social-media ministry. We did this by visiting the different social-media platforms to see which members were using social media the most. Then, I simply met with these persons, cast the vision of a social-media ministry, and invited them to use their gifts. If you are a pastor, then you already know your plate is full; therefore, this ministry should be led by gifted and talented laypeople. Encourage them to post during the streaming broadcasts to get people posting, sharing, liking, and tagging one another. Your social-media ministry leader(s) can also respond to comments and welcome guests who are tuning in. This gives you an opportunity to follow up with people, answer their questions, and share with them your vision.

- Offer clear ways for online viewers and participants to communicate with you. The goal is always to create deeper relationship for spiritual impact and development.

- Following any streaming worship service or event, review it thoroughly to see if there is anything that can be corrected or improved upon the next time.
- *Always* be prepared to receive and respond to positive and constructive feedback.

So, Does Social Media Work for Churches?

The short answer to this question is "Yes." In our first week of widespread public awareness of the COVID-19 pandemic in 2020, when we were first forced to worship exclusively online, our Facebook statistics indicated that we reached 1,100 people, with 1,800 video views and 2,100 engagements.[1] This was more than twice what our prior normal attendance had been. And for weeks after this, we saw these numbers steadily increase. This sort of increase in the numbers of weekly worship participants was the common experience of churches all over the planet, and especially those who were ready to offer a compelling online experience. Globally, even as a number of people disengaged during 2020, additional numbers of people reengaged in this fashion, often creating net gains in church engagement.

We live, increasingly, in a digital world. People are online, steadily increasing in their daily screen time and searching for experiences that offer hope. It is up to us to provide that hope. We can do it by connecting well through social media. In these next years beyond the pandemic, as people feel safe coming back to gather in person, many people will choose to continue worshiping online—at least some of the time. More of our first-time guests will get their first taste of our church online—before, perhaps, deciding to come join us in an in-person gathering. The church, as we have known it, will be significantly different. We must all recognize that we must be prepared for this by making effective use of our social media platforms to meet this new season of connecting with people in new and relevant ways.

21

THINKING TWO TRACKS: DIGITAL AND IN-PERSON

Paul Nixon

Most of the changes currently occurring in the life of worship communities were underway before 2020; they have simply sped up lately.

Derek Jacobs reminded us in the previous chapter that online engagement as a central means of human connection has been increasing for several years. A few years ago, I coached the planting of an online campus for a church in Virginia—a project which, at that time, was truly cutting edge. Now, in the 2020s, having a digital ministry is as basic and universal as having a children's ministry: Only in somewhat rare and niche circumstances would we imagine launching a worship community without either a children's ministry or a digital ministry.

The percentage of Sundays per year on which "regular" participants and members attend worship has been dropping steadily in recent years, as people have become more mobile on weekends. Offering an online option for our weekly worship gatherings may help stop this trend of more sporadic attendance right in its tracks.

My family splits our time between homes in two places. Plus, I typically am on the road working with other churches at least half of the weekends in any given year. So, by the start of 2020, I was down to a total of half a dozen services per year attending worship in either of our home churches. But when we all switched to online gathering in the spring of 2020, my family and I began attending both of our home churches regularly, almost every week! As a result, our sense of connection to the churches we call home has increased.

Honestly, I would rather be in an in-person, physical gathering almost any day. The energy, the human connection, the music—it's all better when it's live, in the room! But there are a lot of days in most people's lives when we just can't get there in-person. An online option is available every hour of every day, week in and week out, to help us stay connected and spiritually energized.

For churches creating a new worship community, it may make sense to launch their online gathering first and then, as momentum builds, add an in-person gathering. There are several reasons for doing it in this order:

- There is no critical mass or minimum attendance required for an effective online ministry, so you can often start up more quickly.
- Weekly momentum can begin to build without having to wait until you are ready to launch a weekly in-person gathering.
- If you are planning to rent space or spend money renovating a space, this spending can be postponed until there are more people onboard to share the costs.
- Online gatherings can be offered in both a real-time and an asynchronous manner. (With recorded presentations, one can access them at any time and at one's own convenience.)
- If you enjoy a particular online experience, you can send a link to invite someone to share in the very same experience without a delay; you do not have to wait until the next gathering—as you would when the meetings are strictly in-person—to extend an invitation.

- There are several easy ways to collect critical contact information from the people who visit your online gatherings and to invite people into future interactions and gentle relationship.
- Online gatherings present a much lower threshold of risk and interest for new people checking out a faith community than asking them to step into an actual room full of strangers.
- As they gain trust in a faith community, online participants often cross over into physical, in-person gatherings.

As Kris Sledge showed us in chapter 10 ("Using Community Conversations to Expand Reach"), we can use online means for gathering people into relationship and conversation, prior to inviting them to worship. Then, in chapter 20 ("Connecting Well in a Digital World"), Derek Jacobs talked about the critical role of social media as a platform for making worship accessible to as many people as possible. In the launch season and beyond, in most settings, online strategies will serve as a complement to live, in-person gatherings.

Even when a church offers a specifically worship-focused online experience, updated each week, the nature and length of the content in the online presentation may be quite distinct from what happens in the physical gathering. A high-energy worship experience can engage most people for sixty to ninety minutes, when they are physically gathered. Online, it is good to think in terms of *half* as long (thirty to forty-five minutes). This means either editing the physical gathering's sermon down or separately preparing a shorter version to offer online.

But there is so much more that can happen online beyond the streaming of worship content. For example:

- interactive worship with small gatherings and live chat/discussion of the scripture or topics;

- small-group interaction that picks up on themes that were prominent in the streaming worship experience; some of these circles could work to organize action in response to the Word;
- interview shows, focused on topics and persons of community interest;
- short, daily devotional thoughts and podcasts, exploring ideas that flow from the previous Sunday's worship theme;
- prayer time and one-on-one conversations that can be scheduled or initiated by those who view streaming content; and
- links to related content (music, talks, video clips, and so on) that is not used directly in the streaming-worship experience; most of this will be related content that has been produced somewhere other than your church.

It is, therefore, reasonable that there would be an online producer who would be a part of any worship-design team. And this person would build his or her own team, as any other member of the worship-design team would. Though it is a good practice for pastors to have a prominent visibility online, they need help; maintaining an online ministry is more than most pastors can do alone.

Whatever platform you choose for your online offerings, the links to them should be easy to find on the home page of your church's website. The harder it is for me to find the door to online worship and other experiences, the less likely I am to enter. Make it easy. Post the dates and themes clearly for each link to worship and other offerings. If I like what I find, I may wish to come back and check out your church's content from previous weeks; please make it easy for me to do so!

Also, make it easy and inviting for me to give feedback, even if it's just to respond to a fun community-wide question. For example: What is your favorite way to keep cool in summertime? What is your favorite band or vocal group, either from the current music scene or prior years? These are easy icebreaker sorts of questions, enabling baby steps in engagement.

After people have responded once, the chances of further interaction go up for them. So, make it easy and fun for anyone to get started.

If you wish to host group conversations, it is important that the facilitator of any conversation be trained in how to facilitate, and in what to do when a group will not talk, when one person dominates, or when someone becomes upset or angry. Getting the proper training for everyone involved is crucial. Do not throw anyone into a role of leadership—online or otherwise—without equipping all leaders for their tasks! They may have led in other churches, but your church is different, and you want to be sure that they understand how to represent and attend to your church's core values in any online engagement.

Finally, whatever hospitality and follow-up expected at your church when you are gathered physically, look for ways to do something comparable online. The point of hospitality is to help people feel welcome, to give them clues that you are interested in them personally, and to make it easy for them to make friends and form relationships at your church. An interactive place is a sticky place and a compelling place, to which we are likely to return. The most basic rule is that we should never fail to respond when a person gives us even a sliver of personal information. Think of it like a tennis match: When people give you any information, they are serving the ball over the net to you; then, it is up to you to return serve by hitting the ball back to them, putting it once again in their court. There are so many different ways to respond to people; you can vary it by week and alternate different people to make the response, but in no case is it acceptable to ignore someone who is giving you information that they exist.

Keep in mind that some of your online participants may live several miles away from your main church facility, and so it's possible you will rarely see them at your in-person gatherings, unless it's one taking place within their local community. Other folks may live just down the street but will still choose online gathering as their primary mode of connection. Regardless of their addresses, once people start hanging out with you online, take them seriously, and seek to offer them the next steps in their spiritual journey. In other cases, some people may move away from your geographical area and thus opt to switch to an online connection to remain a part of your church after their move. If several people begin to accumulate in this non-local category, your church may choose to create a team specifically dedicated to serving non-local participants.

Online ministry is developing rapidly all over the world. New best practices will continually emerge, and there will be teaching churches that have discovered excellent ways to engage with folks online from whom we can learn. We will all constantly be learning in the years ahead!

22

DESIGNING THE WORSHIP EXPERIENCE

Craig Gilbert

I f you have made it this far into this book, then I believe that you and your team are serious in your endeavor to launch a new worship community. You are also likely developing a clear plan for what you want from the worship experience. I'll begin here with a foundational metaphor, to which I will refer throughout this chapter. For each of the subsequent steps, I will introduce a new metaphor that I believe best suits the needs of that step. This type of instruction, moving from image to image, may require a bit of imagination for some of the more-literal thinkers on your team, but we are speaking to the artists among you as well! If something seems confusing, reread it and discuss it with one another. This chapter is written specifically to engage each member of your team at different points, and you can help one another understand what I am trying to say.

Basic Elements of Worship

There comes a point in the home-building process when all your dreams and wishes for a new home must be turned into a practical design. Usually, you would consult an architect, whose craft is turning dreams into buildable realities. In this case, you and your fellow team members are the architects and the builders for this dream service.

You have assembled the best team available to you, people who are as gifted as possible in the areas that are needed. Let me offer one caution/ encouragement. When building a house, there is one question against which all construction is checked before it is "nailed down." That question is this: "Is it square?"[1] Only when the building is square will it be able to stand strong. Once the part of the building being constructed is "square," then it is nailed down and the builders can move on with confidence to the next elements. There is nothing more disappointing in building a structure than to be far along in the process only to discover that something nailed down earlier was not actually square. Often there is no way around this mistake. The only reasonable resolution is to tear everything apart to that point, "square it up," and begin building again. This has happened to me, a non-builder, on more personal projects around my home over the years than I can count. Therefore we need to be careful each step of the way to make sure that our decisions are square with our objectives. So, how do we know when our worship construction is "square?"

Throughout your journey of launching a new worship community, your team has been working toward discerning God's plan for the worship service. In chapter 2 ("Why Start a New Gathering?"), you were prompted to reflect deeply upon why you are creating it. With chapters 5 ("Focusing on a Particular Set of People") and 6 ("Building Bridges with the People We Seek"), you sharpened your focus on the group of people for whom this service will be designed. Then, in chapter 12 ("What Do We Want People to Experience in Worship?"), you worked through what you wanted these people to experience in the worship gathering. All the way through the process, you have asked God, through prayer, to be present in and to guide your planning. So now, on this basis, your worship structure can be considered "square" at each decision when you make sure that your plans for worship align perfectly with God's plans, as revealed in your prior work. Remember, no amount of paint or beautiful artwork can strengthen a crooked wall when the storm winds begin to blow.

Worship Content

You will seek to build your worship service to include all the actions of worship that you have envisioned for this new gathering. Going back to our home-building metaphor, these actions are like dedicated rooms in your new worship home, where specific actions will take place. Examples include songs, the sermon, the offering, prayer time, the greeting, and so on. Make a list of these actions, in no particular order. Many teams will try to order worship actions at the same time they are making a list of them. However, before you try to put your list in any certain order, you must first decide whether everything on your list is even needed. Resist the temptation to put the items in a specific order. Keeping them listed in a random fashion will actually make it easier to take the next step, which is applying the question, "Is it square?" As I indicated above, making it "square" means looking at each worship action for what it is and checking it against what you believe God's vision is for your worship service. Talk about each individual action, and decide now how each one specifically fits into—or does not fit into—what you believe God is calling you to do to engage your chosen community in worship. If an action does not fit, could it be reimagined so that it fits better? Just because a particular action is "something we have always done in worship" does not mean that it automatically squares up with your new plan. Why take the time and effort to build a room you do not need, that doesn't fit, or that won't be effective? Another way of putting it is this: Imagine that your family has a much-loved old couch, but the couch is worn out. You wouldn't build a new family room designed around your worn-out sofa, right?

For every action of worship you are considering including, ask yourselves questions such as, "What would this look like/sound like/feel like in our worshiping community?" "How would this specific action bring us closer to God or God closer to us?" You might start with an action you think is obvious to be included—such as the sermon, for instance—and then run it through what I call "the squaring process." This is a series of questions like those outlined above intended to bring you clarity regarding how the worship action you are considering will meet God's expectations for your new service and how it will be used in that service, as well. Follow this process for every action item on your list, from those that seem the most obvious for inclusion to the ones you think may be the most disposable. As you go through this process, your questions will get better, and your answers will have stronger convictions. Unless you and your team are incredibly good planners, there may be some worship actions on your list that you will ultimately discard or significantly change. This process of close examination may reveal places where you need to add something you had not previously considered.

Let me give you an example of what I am talking about. One item that many churches struggle with in worship is announcements. Many churches I work with ask, "What worshipful role does stopping to talk about upcoming events play in the service?" My answer is to start asking them questions:

1. Why do we do announcements in the first place?
2. Are we interested only in increasing attendance to other events?
3. Is it because it makes some people feel that their event is more important because it was announced in worship?
4. Are announcements even effective for their intended purpose?
5. Is there some way an announcement could be considered an act of worship?

These are the types of questions you must ask regarding each action you are considering as you attempt to determine whether it is square with the intentions and goals of your service.

After addressing these questions, these worship design teams knew that the typical approach to placing announcements in worship was not square with their intentions. Instead of taking time at the beginning or the middle of a service to announce what was coming, they decided to move the announcements to the end of the service as part of the benediction or sending forth, framing them as part of their sending-out-into-ministry-and-into-the-community time as a church. Upcoming events became opportunities to respond to God's call to serve, rather than simply advertisements for various ministries. This allowed the action of announcements to continue as part of the worship service, but it was now contextualized in such a way that it was square with the worship community's goal to see its congregation active in service to others (and to be honest, God's goal of making disciples). They even took the next step in completing the vision by including "praise reports" prior to prayer time. These reports allowed them to celebrate the ways God moved in events that were previously simply "announced" and forgotten.

That, of course, is just one example. Your team will need to examine and carefully consider all your actions in this way. As you do, you will be ready to begin to build your worship service.

Now that you have your list of actions that make up the content of your service, let's look at their order.

Worship Order

The best way to think about creating the order of your worship service is to think about a story. In a good story, each event logically leads to the next event, and so on, until the story is told. You may order one service differently from the next; they don't have to follow a predictable pattern.

Many worship theologians and scholars compare worship to a story or a conversation: Each action leads to the next, until the whole story is told.[2] The best tool I have found for this process is to think of the order of worship as the outline for a story. After you build the order in outline form, then the actual story line—where it begins, where it climaxes, and how it ends—should be obvious to anyone looking at it, even though the details of the story have yet to be filled in. If you do not understand what I mean, try the following team-building exercise:

1. Pick out any fiction book that no one on your team has read; short books with clear stories work best.
2. Assign a different chapter to each team member, and ask them to read their assigned chapters. However—and this is of key importance—*do not let your team members see which particular chapter number they have! Give each person only the content of his or her chapter, without any indication of where that chapter fits into the overall story.* (Begin with the first chapter, and make assignments in sequential order until each member has a chapter.)
3. Now, gather your team, and as each member reveals the contents of his or her chapter, see if the team members can arrange and/or rearrange themselves to tell the story in the proper order.

The point is not the difficulty of the task but the thought process needed. Actually, understanding of this part of worship design should be an "Oh wow, that was easy. But, I never thought about like that" moment. This can be an incredibly fun activity that will clearly demonstrate the need for every part of your service to be in the right order for telling the story of God in worship that you are trying to tell in any given service.

This outline you have created, the "Order of Worship," can be extremely adaptable. It can be revised and filled in each week with the specific content—such as songs, prayers, scriptures, and so on—that you need specifically for that week. This method allows you to tell new stories about God each week. You can change the order as needed if you wish to tell a new story in a different way. You can even create templates for two, three, or four common orders of worship, deciding from week to week which one will work best.

And always remember, if you need to add a new worship action or take one away, you can go back to the content questions you used earlier in this chapter to make your evaluation: "What would this look like/ sound like/feel like in our worshiping community?" and "How would this specific action bring us closer to God or God closer to us?" The order of worship is simply an arrangement of the actions you have decided you need to include to be "square" with God's expectations for worship that week. There may be times when you want to change how you tell the story. In those cases, you can bring in a substitute action, remove one or more actions to create more space in the service, or add something different to create a new dynamic. Remember: *Having an order of worship does not mean you are stuck with that version of the story forever*. It just means that whatever story you are telling, you are telling it with purpose and clear direction that makes the worship easy to follow and understand by everyone who joins the experience.

Worship Flow

This is the final part of building an excellent and completely engaging worship experience for your congregation. Moving from action to action in a way that keeps the congregation engaged throughout the service is called *flow*. The goal is for the end of each action to *flow* as seamlessly as possible into the next from the first action to the last.

To create this flow, transitions must be considered just as carefully as the action itself. The concept of being "square" is just as important in transitions as it is in actions. If words will be used to move from one action to another, they must remain "square" to the overall service. I have seen many wonderful services, full of meaningful worship actions, fall apart because the words used in a transition were not thought out but dropped in "off the cuff" and were completely out of line with the rest of the service. The same is true for services where other types of transitions received little to no consideration. Movement of people, lights, turning microphones on and off, all must be considered to have a great flow in worship. Not taking this final step can result in a choppy service, full of holes, awkward silences, and a basic failure to know what is next. This can embarrass participants and leave the congregation looking toward the floor, or worse, headed for the door.

All-Inclusive Worship Planning

Finally, great worship planning and design includes having *everyone* involved in making the worship service come to life. In church after church where I have coached on worship design, I am amazed at how team members who operate the ministries that are considered ancillary— areas such as sound, lights, video, decoration, and ushers or greeters, for example—are often the last people to know what is going on in the service. Including these ministries in the worship-planning process will often help you to stay on track in meeting your overall worship goals.

Bringing any of the worship actions in your service to life might be enhanced by input from the ministries that can make those actions look and sound good. The area of worship flow is greatly influenced by the ability of sound, light, and video to enhance the movement from one action to the next. Your planning team might even think of the greeters and ushers as the cover of the book containing the story you are about to tell. I have been able to create amazing worship experiences by giving greeters and ushers specific things to say to people as they come into the church.

What I hope you have seen in this chapter is that good worship planning involves more than picking a song or two, saying a prayer, reading a scripture, taking up an offering, preaching a sermon, and then going home. There are thousands of churches for whom that list is exactly what a worship service looks like, Sunday after Sunday, year after year. This is your chance to do something different and—more importantly—something that is clearly directed to and designed specifically for your new, budding congregation.

23

SELECTING MUSIC
AND MUSICIANS

Craig Gilbert

By this point, you may be saying, "Finally, *music*!" For a lot of us working on the daunting task of starting a new worship service, music is where we are tempted to start. Often, the vision of the new service is formed around music that is distinctive from that of other services and churches. If you have skipped to this chapter because this is what you are most interested in, I encourage you to please return to earlier chapters in this book and read the chapters relevant to your task as suggested to this point. Don't worry—this chapter will still be here when you get here again!

Choosing Music

You likely made decisions (or certain assumptions) about the style of music you'd prefer for your worship service long before you came to this chapter. In fact, wanting a new musical expression for your congregation may have been the impetus for deciding to start a new service in the first place. A discussion about choosing the music for your worship service may even have begun with a list of favorite styles, songs, and artists compiled by several members of your team; this has been the starting point for untold numbers of new worship services. Some of these new services succeed; many fail. Regardless, be aware that on its own, music is rarely a solid reason for starting a new service. (And I say this as a church musician.)

WARNING: Now is not the time to abandon all the hard work you have done to build a worship service for the new people you are hoping to attract by beginning with *your* favorite music or by assuming you know precisely the style and range of music that is appropriate for this service.

As you have already discovered, it can be hard to let go of things that you hold to be tried and true when it comes to worship. It can be especially hard to let go of music that has carried you through tough times, allowed you to express your joy, or opened your soul to God's presence in worship. But you are creating a new worship community to minister to people who are not like you. This means there is a very good possibility that they will want to express their feelings toward God and hear about God in a musical language that is different from your own. In fact, you should be prepared for the possibility that they will want to worship with *music you never thought would be right for worship or even knew existed.*

Hopefully, you have people on your team who reflect the demographic you are seeking to reach. And hopefully, they are ready to contribute their thoughts and beliefs about music to the process. If not, then you need to sit down with people in the community who represent the demographic you are trying to reach and get their input. Ask them to bring in examples of the kind of music they really love. The music could be sacred or secular, as long as they find that it personally takes them to a place of spiritual focus. As a group, take time to listen to this music together, and then have these new folks describe why this music invites them to worship God. In my experience, listening to the music together and hearing the hearts of others spoken out loud has helped my teams to better understand the *why* of the selection process.

It is not necessary to pick specific music right now. It is simply important to, as a team, finalize the style or range of styles and locate a variety of examples so that you can begin the next part of the process: selecting a music leader.

Selecting a Music Leader

As with the music itself, it's possible you have already decided whom you will ask to be the music leader for this service. The person leading the music team, group, or choir is one of the most important positions you will be selecting, as it applies to the success of your new worship service. This person is the musical "expert" who will bring the experience and overall feel to the rest of your musicians and, in a very tangible way, to the whole service. You need to find the best fit for your worship service and your church. If you begin this selection process with an open mind, you will be more likely to find the right person whom God has called to lead the music in your new service.

This person may be already in your church. More than likely, though, you will need to consider people beyond your current church membership. Please try to avoid simply handing the responsibility to a person in your church who may be willing but who lacks the skill and/or authenticity to pull it off. And, no, simply being willing to learn is not an acceptable substitution for actual skill and experience when it comes to the style of music you have selected. What may seem the easier path now is likely to cause you a lot of pain later. Choosing the wrong person for the job, no matter the reason, may even sink all the hard work you have done to get your worship service going. Yes, this selection is *that* important; oh, the stories I could tell!

When looking outside of your church for a music leader, advertising locally can be effective. Depending upon the style you have selected, you might try local music stores or schools. Another source, one that is often overlooked, is other churches. I am not suggesting "stealing" someone else's music leader. However, there may be churches in your area that are so large, they have multiple music teams. Sometimes these churches have persons with solid leadership potential but who are not yet experienced enough to have gotten a chance to lead in such a large church. If you are willing to work in collaboration with this church, you may be able to offer this potential "leader in waiting" an opportunity to lead in your church. This sharing of resources may even result in a wonderful new relationship between your people and another congregation.

There are some serious things to consider when selecting the person to fill the key position of music leader. Here are a few:

1. After you have chosen the range of styles and found some examples of the music you would like to use in worship, you absolutely need to select a leader who is both proficient and *authentic* in that framework. I have experienced more worship services than I can count where the musicians were unable to play the music style chosen with any authenticity. It is not just about skill; it is about having a natural feel for the music. Think about this like a language: A person speaking in a second language is rarely as strong as people speaking in their native tongue. The same principle is true in music.

2. That being said, *do not* fall into the age/gender/ethnicity trap. A lot of churches begin the process of choosing a music leader by listening to the music and then deciding what the leader should look like. Great leaders/players/singers may not be given a real chance because they do not look the part according to the team's expectations. This happens all the time, especially in this image-first culture. Don't let appearances keep you from checking out qualified

candidates. There are so many examples of musicians who fell in love at some point in their life with a kind of music and crossed stereotypical boundaries to become excellent in that style, even though they may not "look the part."

3. Finally, be mindful that *your leader is not necessarily the person who will be out front.* Read that again, and let it sink in. This may be something you have never considered. Do not just default to how you have seen things done online or in other churches. Many times, the worship music leaders never step up to a microphone. Instead, they may choose the music, coordinate the rehearsals, coach the worship team, encourage the members, and do all the things a great worship leader does *except* actually lead worship. I have recently seen this method applied even in the world of traditional-style worship, where either the choir director or chief accompanist does not hold the actual "music leader" position. In such a case, these churches may have great organists and/or choir directors, but their music leader is someone else entirely. In today's world, be open to nonstandard possibilities and options.

The Rest of the Story

Once you have selected your music leader, then that person will be your go-to person for all final music selections. This will be the person who will take the results of your team decisions about music and begin selecting musicians and music that will provide an effective fit. Of course, until you have established a clear, mutual understanding and a proven track record with your music leader, I am not advocating that you send this person off to do his or her own thing. On the contrary, this leader will become a member of your overall team, so that he or she can hear what the team's expectations are and be a part of making collective decisions until you are ready to let them do more on their own.

24

GETTING READY
TO LAUNCH

Craig Gilbert

Y ou now have your basic order of worship set. You are happy with it. You believe that it tells the story about God that you want to share, in a way that welcomes and engages the people you have invited to come and worship God in your new service, and that it is "square" with where you believe God is calling your church to worship. You have also selected the music you will use and the person who will lead that music in worship.

Congratulations! That is an amazing accomplishment. Now, it is time to see if the order of worship and the resulting worship experience you have created will actually do what you have planned for them to do.

You will need to stage a demonstration service. Planning your first "demo" service is an amazing experience. Much like new restaurants will have a "soft opening" before their grand opening, you are going to design and offer a demo service as practice for the real thing. There is so much expectation; hope; anticipation; and, yes, pressure, that your team will be ready to bust. But remember (as the voice of the Emergency Broadcast System used to tell us, long ago): "This is a test. This is only a test." Let the process grow organically. Be open, and see where God is leading you.

Let everyone have a chance to lean in and see what can be done. If you have made it this far in the process of launching a new worship community, you should by now have everything you need to produce a wonderful worship experience. You will have a chance to reflect and refine after this test service. But you need to start somewhere, and now it is time put the process you have devised through its paces.

Worship-Planning Time

You know how to have a great meeting (see chapter 19, "Running Good Meetings"). Gather your team, pull out that order of worship, and plan your first demo service. *Hint*: If you go ahead and plan the service that you want to use as your first public service, then you will be getting a great head start by using it as your demo service. Go through every worship action, and select great content that fits the needs of the service. Now, look at the worship flow, and plan those transitions so that everything moves well from one worship action to the next.

Take It for a Test Run

Time to move this service to the actual venue where it will take place for a first run-through. In show business, we call this a dress rehearsal. Worship is not show business, of course, but it involves performance and lots of transitions, so having a dress rehearsal is essential. This run-through should include everyone needed to make the service happen. Those who are helping to present the service will be at work, doing their jobs. Those team members who are part of only the planning process will be sitting in the room, worshiping with the team, but also writing down their observations about how the run-through is going. Sound, lights, video: Everything needs to be included for evaluation. It is also very important that this service be streamed online in a way that enables you to test your streaming capabilities. It should be run on a test site that can be viewed only by your team, since you are not yet ready to go fully public. Complete a full run-through of the service. After this first run-through, you may want to take a break, get some feedback from your selected observers, write down some notes, make some adjustments, and then have a second full run-through before you call it a day.

Did you get all of that done? Then, congratulations—you just finished your first effort at your new worship service!

Time for Another Meeting

Gather the team and begin discussing how everyone felt about the run-through. Everyone should get a chance to talk. Be sure to begin with what went right: Where did things go exactly as planned? Where did you experience some great surprises? Now, where were there some areas that you think need to be improved? What can you do to make the service better? Be specific in your comments, questions, and responses. These discussions among your team members should be informed by things people remember from the run-through or from notes that were taken. Once this discussion runs its course or you reach the time limit you have set for it, take a break, and prepare to come back for part two.

Time to "Go to the Tape"

Ask any professional athlete where they spend most of their training time. Their answer may surprise you: It is watching game playback. (We used to call this "watching game film" or "watching game [video]tape.") This is where the athletes compare what they think they remember about the game to the playback of the actual game recording that shows them exactly what happened. While they watch, their coaches point out specific areas where the athlete can improve. This learning experience can be difficult, but it is necessary. Here is an inconvenient truth: The game recording doesn't lie!

Sit down together as a team, and watch the demo service run-through from your streaming archive. This will provide three critical components:

1. *Truth*: The first thing is that you will be able to observe how you look and sound. Often, people on a stage think they are being expressive and inviting; but afterward, when they see themselves on video, they discover otherwise. Other things, such as worship flow, clarity of the story, and more, can also be accurately reviewed by watching the video.

2. *Stream*: This playback viewing will also allow the entire team to assess the critical component that is your online presence. Everyone will have a chance in this process to talk about how your worship presentation sounds, looks, and even feels in the online world. Camera angles, the placement of people on the platform or stage, the lighting, and the quality of the video stream are all technical aspects that need to be reviewed, critiqued, and adjusted as necessary.

3. *Team Building*: Doing this run-through review as a team, especially at the beginning of this process, is *critical*. It allows everyone to see how interdependent the entire process is for everyone. It also gives an opportunity for everyone to hear feedback together, both the praises and the critiques. But do remember, all feedback needs to be encouraging.

Do It Again!

The next step in the process is this: Take all the feedback your team has provided, go back to step one, and do it all again. You'll want to keep going through this process, honing this new worship service, until it is exactly as you need it to be.

The process in this chapter can and should be used periodically for evaluation purposes throughout the year. A minimum expectation would be to stage a quarterly run-through of all the steps in this chapter. This will provide you with invaluable information, feedback, and team-building opportunities.

I realize that the steps in this process may sound technical, even clinical. You may not be used to thinking of worship preparation in this way. Many times, when I teach this method, I am asked questions such as, "Where is there room for the Holy Spirit in all of this?" "If you prepare to this level, how is God supposed to get in a word?" "This seems like you are producing a show; how is that spiritual?"

The truth is that God is present in all this planning. I believe that the Holy Spirit is guiding our choices. When we review what we have done, the Holy Spirit reveals to us where we can strive yet harder for excellence and where we can celebrate. The potential misunderstanding here is the notion that if we are too practical and prepared, God will not be present. For perspective, I go to the Bible, to the books of Kings and Second Chronicles, and I see the detail that goes into the preparation of the Temple for worship, all the intricate and specific details of how worship is to be performed. I read about the calling and preparation of the musicians and others in the service to worship in the Temple. I believe this is proof that God honors our work. God desires our best efforts.

And I know from experience that God fills our worship offering with God's Spirit and uses it for God's glory. So many times, I have prepared a worship service just as I outlined above, only to experience that when we worshiped with others using our plan, God showed up in unexpected ways. Our mistake is to believe that our preparations somehow limit God. If that were true, there would not be much reason to worship.

Once you have gone through this process—perhaps several times— and you believe you have designed and successfully executed your worship service just as you have planned, then you are ready to launch. Just know that things may be difficult at first, as you try to build a service week in and week out. But trust in your planning, and you will find comfort and strength in the knowledge that God honors your work.

25

OFFERING WORLD-CLASS HOSPITALITY

Paul Nixon and Sandy Gutting

Paul: Sandy, twenty years ago, you and I met during the launching of a new worship community in the neighborhood where you live. I met you at a block party that preceded the actual worship launch. You jumped right in, offering hospitality to your neighbors even before you joined the church, months before you came on board our staff as the director of hospitality. When I used to walk through those doors of our lobby on Sunday mornings, it was like walking into a wall of love and good mojo. I know you had a lot to do with that, so I thought we might unpack exactly how a launch team can create that kind of atmosphere.

Sandy: Paul, those years were so much fun. One big key was how that hospitality got into the DNA of the place.

Paul: How do you get hospitality into a launch team's DNA?

Sandy: You start as early as you can. You start with the planting pastor and other key leaders. They have to live it, and then good habits should be practiced in the earliest gatherings of the small groups and the launch team. From the very earliest days, the planting pastor and other leaders should be on the lookout for persons who have the passion and skills to welcome others. Recruit them early on, and empower them to do their magic.

Paul: So, we are looking for individuals who have hospitality in their blood—people for whom this is a gift. What are the telltale signs of these potential leaders?

Sandy: They smile. They pay attention to the people around them, especially the new people. They take the initiative to introduce themselves. They are positive people who warm up a room. And they are appreciative. They say, "Thank you."

Paul: It seems that there are always a few carriers of this kind of DNA on every good hospitality team. But they also have to be organized, right?

Sandy: Yes. Or I might instead use the word *intentional*. Intentionality grows out of their personal passion that people should be made to feel at home. So, they commit to *seeing to it* that certain things happen for every person who walks in the door. Smiles and eye contact must happen. Greetings must happen. Attention must be given to each person, appropriately. Positivity must be felt in the room. Appropriate refreshments must be prepared and served. And warmth must be extended—not only to guests, but to the hospitality team itself. As assignments are made and reminders are sent, we have to treat each other with TLC. We can't go around demanding things of our team members and volunteers. We have to respect that they each have different capacities for helping. And things sometimes happen in their life that have an impact on this.

Paul: Let's imagine a worship community with 200 attendees. How many folks will we need to have on our hospitality team for 200 attendees?

Sandy: Okay, let's see . . . We will assume that we have three entrances. And we need to have two greeters at each entrance. If there is any kind of long hallway to the children's area or the worship area, you will need someone who can serve as a guide in that space. Then, we need a refreshment team, an information-area attendant, greeters handing out bulletins at the entry into the worship area, and ushers to help with the offering and with seating. Add in a pool of volunteers for special events. I would say you will need to have at least twenty hospitality-team members present on any given Sunday, but also another thirty hospitality-team members who can be assigned to serve occasionally. Some people like to serve every week, while others prefer to volunteer once a month. So, we are up to fifty people in the total pool. That comes out to *one hospitality team member for every four people in attendance.*

Paul: That is very helpful: a one-to-four ratio of hospitality team members to total attendees. That is probably more people on the hospitality team than some of our readers expected. And in all fairness, some readers are planning and dreaming for fifty total worshipers, not 200, so they can scale these numbers accordingly! I recall that you and your team often had people helping out in small ways by their third time in attendance.

Sandy: Some people are ready to connect, you can just tell. And what better way to meet people and make friends than to help as a greeter or to work with a team serving refreshments?

Paul: If I know six people by name and they know me by name, I am likely going to feel like I belong—which means that I am going to stick around. Getting me into the hospitality-team rotation is an easy way to Velcro me into the fellowship. Relationships are sticky!

Sandy: Exactly!

Paul: Food and coffee cost money to provide, and they take time to purchase and prepare. Are they absolutely necessary?

Sandy: Yes. The early Christian church never met without eating and drinking. It's a vital part of how we do community. Having food and drinks naturally makes people relax and feel at home. It encourages conversation. Refreshments are really a tool for relationship building. And, yes, it takes a lot of work. But it also gives more opportunities for incorporating people onto the team. Done right, with excellence, it can be work turned into fun.

Paul: Just before the COVID-19 pandemic set in and hugs became dangerous, I attended a church where I had the experience of walking into that "wall of love" again. Even though I have often warned against overdoing the welcome at the front door of the church, this young man was giving out hugs, and it was the most endearing thing. I felt like the prodigal son on the front porch of the father's house! It was a bit of a sideways hug, not very long; but it told me that I was walking into a different kind of place than, say, a supermarket or the movie theater. I thought about that greeting all week long, and I decided that it worked well in the cultural context of that community. I can imagine some places where it would just scare people to death. So, the level of hospitality has to be contextual, doesn't it?

Sandy: Yes. We need to respect all people for who they are. There will be a range of personalities within any one community. Some will be introverts. We can read their body language, if we are paying attention. One-on-one, quiet conversation is much more comfortable for some people than loud, chaotic conversation. But this also varies from one neighborhood to the next. All over the world, there are different social rules from one place to the next about how men relate to women, how children relate to adults, how younger people relate to older people, whether and how much eye contact is appropriate, and on and on we could go. This is why it is best for someone who is local to help organize the hospitality your church offers in ways that make sense for that particular context.

Paul: Back to the kid who hugged me. He took a risk, and he pushed to the edge of what would work; but if he was going to err, it was going to be on the side of warmth. He did not play it safe. I think that is what I like most about the way I was greeted. He took a little bit of risk to tell me that I was special and that I was loved. If the worst I can say about a place is that it was really friendly, that's better than saying the opposite.

By the way, you were not the only person in our church who started greeting guests long before you became a member. Do you remember our friend DeWitt?

Sandy: DeWitt was a very dear man. He came to us to work off his court-ordered community-service hours due to a driving incident.

Paul: He didn't know we were a church at first—and he didn't like churches. When he figured it out, he was disappointed. But he needed the service hours, and he stuck around. And we had all our community-service workers help out on Sunday.

Sandy: He really had the hospitality DNA we were talking about earlier. He loved people and made people feel welcomed. He had run a diner for many years and had built a business doing this. So, we gave him bulletins and designated him a worship greeter.

Paul: He would listen to the worship service, sitting in a chair just outside the door. One day, I noticed he had moved his chair inside the door. Then, on another day, we had given an invitation to those gathered to come down to the front of the church and pray. DeWitt said, "I'm going down there, but I am not joining this church." It went on like this, until he became a lay preacher and then served as the leader each Sunday at another ministry site. That ministry journey started when we embraced God's gift of hospitality in him.

Sandy: DeWitt was also our Chef at Café 98, our Tuesday-night community dinner.

Paul: He could not believe that we were trying to take reservations for a mid-week dinner. He told me that if restaurants on Highway 98, where we were located, required reservations, they'd all go out of business!

Sandy: He understood the importance of asking people to help, asking them to serve using their gifts. From peeling potatoes to washing pots and pans to handling the cashbox at the front door, scores of ordinary people were invited to become stakeholders in our church via a weekly community café. We would have between 200 and 400 people come through on a Tuesday evening over the course of two-and-a-half hours. DeWitt would wear his chef hat and walk around the room, greeting every person.

Paul: Those Tuesday-evening dinners at Café 98 became a weekly practice drill for the ministry required of us in 2005, following Hurricane Ivan, when one-fourth of our community members found themselves homeless—you included! At that point, our church became a shelter, a community dining hall, and a place where people could cry on one another's shoulders and also find purpose helping their neighbors, even as their properties lay in ruins. When the winds died down, some of our folks just broke into the kitchen and started cooking anything they could find for their neighbors. It was beautiful; no permission needed.

Paul: Is there anything else you think we should mention—perhaps about the room setup where hospitality occurs?

Sandy: Whenever possible, you need to have an open area with natural light and good lighting/fixtures. If there is seating, it should be arranged to encourage conversation. There should be an area designated for refreshments and welcoming. I would suggest working with someone who is a professional or who has proven decorating skills to furnish the space. Think about the space in terms of logistics, the ease of serving people, and cleanup. But also, think about the person who will be showing up there for the very first time. You want the space itself to convey to them: "We were expecting you! You are special. We are so glad you are here."

Paul: Several years after you and I worked together, Sandy, I served as an advisor for the planting of a worship community where I had nothing to do with anything happening onstage. So, I helped as a greeter. I would add a new row of chairs in the back of the room when a crowd would arrive ten minutes after the scheduled start time. And, I will say, that was one of the most joy-filled jobs I ever had in ministry: standing in the space where we get to welcome God's children home. Thanks for all you taught me across the years about how do hospitality well!

Sandy: We had fun, Paul, even in the crazy moments!

26

ONBOARDING NEW PEOPLE INTO COMMUNITY

Dan Pezet

First Church had a problem: They had many first-time visitors, but only a few of them turned into second-time visitors. To correct the problem, the staff read several books on making first-time visitors feel welcome, and they made changes to offer excellent hospitality. They added parking-lot greeters, great signage, information centers, people who offered tours, and designer coffee. While these elements of hospitality were helpful, visitors still came in and went out as if through a revolving door. First Church began to realize that hospitality and quality worship content were not enough to help people feel they belonged as part of the faith community; First Church had an onboarding problem.

Onboarding someone into your new faith community involves more than welcoming visitors. You can invite visitors to your home, offer great hospitality, and they may still leave as visitors. *Onboarding* goes much deeper: It is a spiritual process of transformation that takes a person from being a visitor to a being embraced as a committed member of the faith community. This transformative work is accomplished through building relationships and helping people connect to church life in meaningful ways.

Your new worship community is all about being in healing relationship with God and with one another. Such relationship is a natural expression and by-product of our faith. And it is our mission to help more people experience the joy of discovering such relationships.

Unfortunately, many of our churches have not yet adapted to our rapidly changing context to be successful at the relationship work required. In some cases, they have become inwardly focused and have forgotten how to make new friends in the community. In other cases, they just do not have the right on-ramps in place. In the late twentieth century, the worship service often functioned as the main on-ramp for a new person into the life of the church; but today, the best on-ramp might precede significant participation in worship or involve a quite distinct experience after a few weeks of worship attendance. And even churches that had excellent onboarding just a few years ago have had to rethink everything to account for the massive increase in online gathering and interaction.

On-Ramps for Today's Church

Starting in the years following World War II, a clear pattern emerged in many American churches for how people got started in church and progressed toward deeper involvement. Often, it began with people "moving their membership to a church" as early as the first Sunday they attended any gathering there. The progression would run like this: worship attendance ➡ Sunday school/women's group/men's group/youth group ➡ serving church/community.

This old pattern of getting involved in church is mostly gone. People now connect with a church *at any point* along the discipleship pathway. The younger the person is, the more likely his or her discipleship journey will work in the opposite direction of the old pathway. A person may hear about the church serving the community in some way; join in that activity; and, from there, be invited to connect with a small group and then worship. And people may start that process at any point these days: serving church/community ➡ small group ➡ worship ➡ membership covenant (maybe).

After looking more closely at the patterns of the few second-time visitors we had at First Church, we discovered that many of them had been involved in the church's food ministry downtown before attending worship for the first time. They were already connected and serving the church before they ever walked through the doors of the physical building. In other words, we were learning that now, more than ever, simply launching a new worship service is not enough to reach new people. A new worship service needs to be accompanied by service opportunities and a network of small groups that reach new people. In this way, church involvement becomes more than simply a worship service; it becomes, truly, a community with worship at its heart.

The rest of this chapter will explore building relationships with new people through the lens of worship, service, and small groups.

Onboarding Through Worship Connections

Many of our traditional onboarding tools revolve around identifying people who are new to the worship service. This usually triggers a series of events to help first-time guests get acquainted with the church, such as giving them a welcome gift; inviting them to fill out information cards; perhaps taking another gift to their home with information about the church; and then some form of pastoral connection with invitations to next steps, which might be a new-member class. These are all still valid methods for connecting with new people, and we should still be doing all these things.

There are three challenges that come with these traditional methods, however. First, people today are much more hesitant to provide personal information than they once were. One study reports that only 33 percent of millennials would be willing to give their email address, and they were even more unlikely to share their home addresses and phone numbers.[1] This means that we need to continually evaluate and adapt the effectiveness of our tools.

Second, many churches miss the key ingredient of traditional follow-up methods: relationship building. Our point in any response to new people should be to build a relationship with them. If they don't know that someone at the church (or better yet, half-a-dozen persons) genuinely like them and are interested in getting to know them better, this will all go nowhere; you cannot fake this.

Third, many churches have not asked how they can offer the same level of responsiveness to newcomers online that they offer to newcomers in-person.

To exemplify how we might change some of these tools to create opportunities for relationship building, let's consider the ministry of greeting. When greeting is done well, the church's lobby can be the most important onboarding opportunity of the whole church system.

Like most churches, First Church worked hard at greeting people on Sundays, but visitors still left feeling like visitors. Door greeters are not usually effective for building relationships, because there is little time for conversation without neglecting the next person coming through the door! To solve this dilemma, in addition to door greeters, assign extra "floating" greeters in the lobby, persons who are naturally extroverted and gifted at connecting with others. These floating greeters might have a conversation with a new person that ends up something like this: "So, you're new in town, and you're a schoolteacher. You need to meet Cindy. She teaches first grade too. Let me introduce her to you." The greeter then goes to get Cindy and makes an immediate connection.

For many people, leading this kind of connecting would feel awkward. A gifted extrovert, though, can cut through the awkwardness and make this a natural and pleasant encounter. Think of it as if you were hosting a party: When throwing a party, it is the responsibility of the host to make connections and introductions between the guests. Likewise, when hosting a worship celebration, it is the responsibility of the church to be the host and to make connections happen in this new faith community.

In addition to the floating greeters, there is another point of opportunity to be found in the church's lobby: the information kiosk. Every time a person goes there to find the answer to a question, it is an opportunity to make a relationship connection. If someone asks about the nursery, this becomes an opportunity to connect the person with the nursery coordinator and/or another parent who has a child in the nursery. I visited a nondenominational church in Indianapolis that did this well. I went to the information desk to see what kind of information they provided there. They gave me a nice, red bag with a T-shirt and a coffee mug inside. A moment later, a very nice young man came over and started talking with me. The conversation was great. I was five minutes into talking with him before I realized that he had intentionally come to speak with me. The effort at conversation was not overdone, but it was intentional. The church had floating greeters who intentionally spoke with people carrying the red bags. Wouldn't it be great if this were so much a part of the culture of the church, that half the members become floating greeters? This kind of thinking can be applied to every part of a hospitality plan, so that the greeting is organized toward relationship building.

In the church's online gatherings in the future, there will be ever-advancing ways to structure people's interactions so that a virtual lobby can be created or, at the very least, a chat function enabled. With such a platform, online greeters can welcome people and have limited and purposeful conversation. (This will be an area of innovation that will move faster in the early 2020s than we could continually edit into a print-edition book! Tag *online greeting* as a topic for watching large and cutting-edge churches and their trends.)

Onboarding Through Service

If I am at someone's house as a guest for dinner and I start to help clear the table after the meal, I am usually told not to worry about it. But when I go to my best friend's house for dinner, he will let me clear the table, and he will be thankful for the help. Serving the church transforms a person from visiting to *belonging*. Part of the onboarding process, then, is helping people find something they are interested in and capable of doing—within the first few weeks after they show up, if possible. When people seek to belong, they want to jump in and make a difference. It is a powerful part of the onboarding process.

Unfortunately, many churches do not invite new people to serve. There seems to be this idea that either no one wants to volunteer until becoming a member; or you must earn the right to volunteer by putting in a year or two of regular worship and maybe joining a Sunday-school class, as a prerequisite to serving. Thriving churches create an atmosphere that invites people to serve right away. Anita Sharron, a hospitality director with whom I once had the pleasure of working, had a special gift for inviting first-time visitors to be a door greeter immediately. She would stand with them and make introductions as people came in. Several years later, I can go back to that church and see several people who were invited to serve that way who are still there and committed to serving (along with many more who have been added since). While I don't think that just anyone can do what Anita did without it seeming weird or awkward, it was never weird when she did it. She certainly showed that inviting people to serve in some capacity should be an early part of the onboarding process.

Consider two different approaches to recruiting volunteers. First, a pastoral announcement: "We still don't have enough volunteers for vacation Bible school. If you are interested, there is a sign-up sheet in the narthex." Second, a personal invitation: "John, our leadership team has been praying about who might be the right person to invite to lead our first-grade vacation Bible school. We feel like the kids would really be blessed to get to know you. We know how much you love your grand-kids, and we think our children need more spiritual granddads. Would you take some time to pray about it and get back to us?" The first invita-tion leaves the work to the new person, who may not feel qualified or even allowed to volunteer. The second invitation does the actual work of onboarding. It builds a relationship, saying the church has a place for you to serve, and it is in connection with your relationship to God.

When onboarding persons into a volunteer opportunity, make sure to connect it to the mission of the church and to each person's personal call. Even folding a printed worship bulletin can be framed as preparing a tool to help people experience God. This is true of every task in the church. These are not just jobs; we toil to fulfill the call God has given us.

To onboard people through service with the community, many churches will have to change their entire approach. Often, "community outreach" involves a closed church team that is doing ministry for a group of people. If there is any collaboration, it is done with other church groups. There is little room for onboarding new people in this kind of closed system. But what if the church took a leadership role in mobilizing all persons of goodwill for serving their neighbors?

One church that was in steep decline took this advice. Their city com-missioner told the members that the city could no longer maintain the park that was a block away from the church, and the commissioner asked them whether the church could help clean it up. Instead of announcing a church-wide cleanup day for church members to come and clean up the park, they distributed door hangers to every house in the surround-ing blocks, announcing that the church was sponsoring a cleanup day at the park. The church invited everyone in the community to help. They provided an inflatable bouncy house for kids, grilled hotdogs, rakes, shovels, gloves, and a dumpster. This declining church of seventy-five weekly worship attendees had almost 400 people come to help clean up the park. This event allowed the members of the church to meet many of their neighbors for the first time and send a message that the church cares about the community.

The key to onboarding new people through service with the community is to *invite the community*! Invite civic groups, school groups, and fire and police departments. Use social media. Train leaders to build relationships with everyone who participates. For people who are new to the church, this is a holy opportunity to put their faith into action. Nonparticipants commonly perceive that the church is hypocritical and does not practice the love that it preaches. The church that serves the community reveals that *this* church is different from that perception. In this sense, the act of leading the community in service is a way of onboarding the entire community.

Onboarding Through Small Groups

Networks of small groups enable relationship building on a level that is not possible during a conventional worship gathering of more than thirty people. When a church adds a second worship service, someone will invariably say, "But we won't be able to know everyone anymore!" Most likely, by this point, the church has already grown beyond the ability of everyone truly knowing everyone else; when pressed, longtime members would have a difficult time naming everyone across the aisle from them. Small groups offer a place where every person can know everyone else. The small group is a place where people find belonging and spiritual companions for their faith journey. Joining a small group is another spiritually transformative moment that takes one from visiting to belonging. From Jesus and his small group of disciples to present-day iterations of small groups, God continues to call people to grow in discipleship in community with other believers.

Effective small groups invite new people to join; and just as it is with every other invitation to participate in church activities, a *personal* invitation works best for small groups. This is a space in which to invite neighbors, parents from the kids' soccer-practice carpool, or friends at work. Intentionally inviting new people will help overcome the tendency for small groups to invite only people who are already deeply committed to the church.

To reach new people, small groups are best when their meetings take place off-site from the church campus. Small groups can meet almost anywhere and are commonly found gathering in homes and restaurants. They can also be formed around activities such as yoga, hiking, golf, and gaming groups. When groups meet beyond the walls of the church, it allows us to connect with people who would be uncomfortable entering a traditional church setting.

There are amazing resources out there on how to develop small groups of all sorts—those in-person, those online, and those that are a hybrid of the two. Let us simply note here that small-group development is as much a part of planting a worship community as developing a music team. Without small groups, the community itself may stay very small and function well as a group or it may grow larger but fall short of truly functioning as a community. You will want to be sure that this task of forming and shaping small groups is included in your ministry-development plan.

Small-group leaders are in a great position to do some of the traditional onboarding of the church. They can make sure that small-group members have information about the larger church connection and the opportunities they will find there. A part of the process of onboarding people into small groups should also be an expectation that the small group will replicate itself at some point. It could be that a group grows to the point where it splits into two, allowing both groups to continue to grow. More commonly (because, usually, the original group of people grows so close together), it will be one or two people from a group who embark on a journey to start a new group.

Measuring the Success of Onboarding

When new people are truly brought onboard, you will see movement. You will see people who entered the faith community through the worship service start to serve as well. You will see people who entered through service to others begin participating in a small group too. This movement is the goal of successful onboarding. Once upon a time, we measured success by counting our members. In recent years, we measured our average weekly worship attendance. In today's church, we can also measure the number of people who have moved from participating in one of the connecting points to two connecting points, three, or more.

There are ways to help encourage movement along the journey. You could invite a small group to serve as parking-lot greeters one Sunday. You could invite the entire worship crowd to take a Sunday to lead a service initiative in the community during the time when they would normally be gathered inside the church. This helps to reinforce the other connecting points, and it invites people to prayerfully consider a deeper connection.

As you begin your new worship community, remember that it is not only about getting people in through the door as first-time visitors. You are creating a community. This community will travel on a spiritual journey together. For it to be a journey, there must be movement. That movement will be centered in a robust onboarding system that builds authentic relationships.

27

CUSTOMIZING CHILDREN'S MINISTRY

Rachel Gilmore

If the community you are trying to reach is full of young families, nothing is more important than your approach to children's ministry. When I started planting a church for young families ten years ago in Virginia Beach, my six-months-old son was the best co-church planter I could have had by my side; Paul Nixon still says little Bennett should have won a Charles Denman Award.[1] We spent our days at parks and playgroups, meeting other young families who were longing for connection with a faith community for their kids to experience love while they received support and encouragement as young parents. As a first-time parent, I was just as concerned as they were about finding a faith community that was both safe and fun for our children.

Cultivating a strong children's ministry first means having a plan for the safety and well-being of the children entrusted to your care. It will not matter how fun, engaging, and innovative your children's activities and programs are if children are hurt or endangered while in your care. The following are tips for safety in children's ministry:

- Ensure that anyone who will be teaching or caring for the children has a background check and that you always have two adults in the room with children of all ages.

- Consider having badges, vests, or T-shirts to easily identify those persons who have been properly vetted to safely and effectively serve in children's ministry each Sunday. My church plant chose to have one paid staff member and one volunteer on Sunday mornings, as opposed to having only volunteers, because the paid staff member could learn the names and needs of each of the children and ensure that the children saw the same friendly face each Sunday to ease "good-bye tears" during drop-off. We viewed paying one staff member for this purpose as an excellent early investment.

- Look at state-mandated regulations for the adult-to-children ratio for each age group, and try to have even lower ratios (a greater number of adults per child) than that which is mandated by the state, to show how much you value the children in your faith community.

- Develop publicity releases and waivers for use when you will be taking pictures of children, as many parents are limiting the digital presence of their children online. Parents do love seeing "proof of life" pictures of their little ones enjoying children's ministry, but they often use a closed group where photos are shared. These groups should be by-invitation-only and updated regularly to limit those who have access to the pictures and videos you take of the children.

- Develop a policy about how you will handle snacks, especially with the rise of incidences of food allergies in children.

- Sanitize classroom toys regularly, and notify all parents if there is an outbreak of highly contagious diseases, such as conjunctivitis.

- Most denominations have some sort of *Safe Sanctuaries*[2] program that can train and equip your pastor and children's ministry leaders and volunteers in best practices in safety with children.

Cultivating a strong children's ministry also means looking at worship through the lens of families and children who haven't been active in a church before. When we launched public worship, the space available to us was a gym, with no separate area for children's ministry. With more children than adults in attendance most Sundays, we intentionally set our worship time for 11:00 a.m. and called it "brunch church," where parents could have quiche and children could have fresh fruit and chicken tenders to eat each Sunday as they sat at round tables with quiet activities such as coloring, modeling clay, and sensory toys. This kept the children engaged while we worshiped together.

It is important to discuss, right from the beginning, whether you will focus on creating space for children to stay in worship with their parents or whether they will be worshiping outside of the main worship space, in their own "children's church." Some parents who work throughout the week want Sundays to be a family affair, where they stay together in worship, while other families want their children to form relationships with their peers, giving the parents time to learn about God in a separate environment. Both approaches are valid, but if you want children to stay in worship, diversify the worship space and make the necessary modifications to the format so that it meets the needs of the variety of ages present.

For children under the age of three,

- add some gliders or rocking chairs for young parents to use while holding their infants; and if you have a separate area for nursing mothers, make sure it is indicated by signage, private, and easy to find; and

- consider having a "pray-ground" space in the main worship area, where children under the age of three can be in worship with their parents and have soft toys to play with.

For preschoolers,

- offer coloring pages that connect with the scripture for that Sunday;
- have a snack area designed for children, with organic juice boxes, an assortment of pre-packaged chips or crackers, and fresh fruit; and
- invite your preschoolers to assist with worship-related activities, such as ushering and greeting. In some church traditions children may serve as acolytes by lighting candles or carrying a cross into worship. Other traditions even allow for participation in roles traditionally kept for adults such as praying and reading scripture. Consider allowing children to serve alongside a parent or family member in the task assigned. This is a great way to help children connect in worship and create bonds between the parent and the child.

For elementary-age children,

- have activity bags with gel fidgets, finger mazes, lacing activities, and printed materials, such as crosswords or coded puzzles, that relate to the Sunday sermon; also, consider adding in "Sermon Notes" handouts for them to fill out as they listen to the sermon; and
- invite the children to serve as acolytes, act as Communion servers, or read prayers or scripture as leaders in worship. This will not only make an impression upon them but it enables the entire congregation to see children engaging publicly in their faith journey.

For middle-school- and high-school-age children,

- offer them the opportunity to help as ushers, act as Communion servers, or read prayers or scripture as leaders in worship;
- invite them to join your band; not only will they have a chance to use their gifts on a Sunday morning but also it will connect them with great mentors among your adult musicians. Make sure your worship leader has a clear policy for how staff and adult mentors will communicate with minors via text or email, and ensure that the parents are informed of the policy as well; and
- make use of their abilities as sound or AV techs. Many teens are more technologically skilled than the adults in worship, so have them assist on Sunday mornings with video or sound after undergoing appropriate training. This will give them skills they can use later in life, they will appreciate the added responsibility, and it will encourage them to attend on a regularly scheduled basis to help worship become a rhythm of their life.

Hopefully, you can find funding for at least a part-time director of children's ministry. Even if you can afford to fund this position for only a few hours weekly, this is still a good investment. Ideally, you will want someone in this position who believes that children are the most important people in the life of the church and who will have a background in education, someone who has the skill to select or create innovative and engaging activities for the little ones at your church. This person will ensure that the children are safe, design ministry that is in sync with the church's philosophy for where and how children will participate, and be thinking constantly about hospitality and communication with parents and children.

Some churches remove age ranges from the doors of their nursery and replace them with signs that have designations such as *Little Lambs* or *Kingdom Kids*; but if you choose this approach, then first-time guests will have no idea where to bring their children. So, the more direct and clear your signage is, the better.

Make sure you have a sign-in system that is easy to follow and understand, and that the parents know how they will be contacted if there is a problem or a concern with their child (such as a text, a buzzer, or a code displayed on the screens during worship). Also, please note that churches full of children are seldom full of judgmental adults yelling at any child who runs in the hallway or leaves sticky fingerprints on a table. Remind the adults in the new worship community about the need to be loving and patient with all the little lives in their midst.

We live in a high-tech society. So, following the worship service, plan to send the parents an email or text with a summary detailing what the children learned about God, along with some age-appropriate ways to extend that learning at home. From spending time riding in the car to mealtimes, bath time, and bedtime, parents want to know how to talk to their children about faith. The more resources you can give them, the more connected they will feel to your faith community.

Offer occasional gatherings for parents where they can talk about godly ways to discipline, to teach children practical life skills, and to guide children of all ages on the use of technology. We implemented a rule in our home that our elementary-age kids could not use tablets or phones from Monday through Friday, so they could disconnect from the digital world around them. It was much easier for them to adjust to this rule because a group of parents at the church implemented it together. This way, it did not seem so "unfair" or "crazy" to our kids. Creating space and ways for parents to learn from one another and talk about the joys and challenges of parenting will only fuel more energy and connection within your church.

In Matthew 18, Jesus tells us that unless we change and become like children, we will never enter the kingdom of heaven. Thriving worship communities today value the presence and insight of children and create opportunities to celebrate and play with childlike joy. Hosting camping trips, hikes, games, picnics, or other events that allow adults and children to laugh and build community together is important in a new worship community. Our church hosted a Pentecost Picnic each year, where the adults compete against the youth in kickball and tug-of-war. Also, we have offered quarterly service projects, where adults and children can serve side by side in ministry. The laughter and sense of connection shared through these events has continued to strengthen our young worship community in its foundational years.

For very small faith communities, sometimes it makes sense to offer a quality children's ministry experience once a month at a time other than Sunday morning, when all hands can be on deck to focus exclusively on having a great children's ministry gathering. This enables the church that has only a handful of children to tell new families, "We do something very special for children here every first Saturday." Neighbors Church in Lincoln, Nebraska, used this strategy in its early years.

Whatever the age range and demographic of your new worship community, you will likely need a strong children's ministry. In the United States, when families who are not attending any church choose to start attending, the number-one reason given continues to be, "For the sake of my kids." Remember that!

28

ALIGNING WITH EXISTING MINISTRIES

Paul Nixon

Whenever a new ministry begins, it is critical that it finds alignment with the larger ministry system in which it is located or hosted. With a new worship community, the chances of losing such alignment are significant. Without such alignment, conflict will occur and possibly also division among people within the church, resulting in a local schism.

What do we mean by "alignment" within a church?

- A common vision of ministry is shared between leaders, groups, and communities under the same organizational umbrella.[1]
- There is a shared language for talking about the faith and the vision of the church.
- There is clarity about how decisions are made—specifically, what kinds of decisions are delegated to leaders at the cellular level and what kinds of decisions are made for the total church (all cells).
- There is agreement on practices or protocols that should be observed at all levels and in all ministry divisions.[2]

- There is a demonstrated respect for other ministries in the church that may serve different primary constituencies, with the leaders of these ministries seen as sisters and brothers in the work of the gospel.

Multisite pastors and large-church pastors have often noted that with new ministries, it is typically easier to deploy leaders who have grown up within the values and practices of that local-ministry system than it is to try to import talented people from outside it. Even if the outside talent comes from the same denomination, they may find points where their instincts or convictions run opposite to the local road rules. Steve Cordell at Crossroads Church in the Pittsburgh area famously has said, "Cut off your arm before hiring a campus pastor from outside your local church."[3] That is hyperbole, and it belies pain from the experience of his church when hiring talented outsiders who are *not quite* on board with the local vision for ministry. When I share that anecdote with seasoned lead pastors of multisite or multiworship community churches, they will all nod knowingly, and they almost always will proceed to recount for me a very painful story about how they learned this the hard way for themselves.

For the purposes of any new worship community, entrust no one, such as a significant vision-caster or preacher, to lead it unless this person has spent *at least a couple of years* within that particular local church system and has shown themselves to be both fruitful in the things they have started and led and also aligned with the senior leadership as a team player.[4] Even if you plan to have one sermon each Sunday provided church-wide by means of a video feed, a non-preaching worship community pastor must be on board with the direction of the messages, the theology, and the vision of ministry.

This alignment is important not only for the pastor/shepherd of the new worship community but also for all leaders in and with the new community. The worship community pastor is responsible for monitoring alignment within their leadership team and immediately addressing *any hint* of non-alignment.

In the first year of the new campus I led at Gulf Breeze United Methodist Church in Gulf Breeze, Florida, the differences in worship style among our campus and the variety of services offered at the mother campus became clear. About three months after we launched worship at the new site, we decided to offer an "Early Christmas Eve service" for people who are out of town with family on December 24. We held this service on a Sunday evening about five days before Christmas, and we invited one of the choirs from the mother campus to join us. Some of our people at the new campus were anti-traditional church to their core. Several of them made disparaging comments about the choral music at this service. It was very important that our campus leadership be united in our response to these remarks. We agreed that we would be kind but firm in saying that we celebrate the diversity of worship styles within our church and that we especially appreciate the fact that it was people with traditional worship instincts who put up a lot of the money to start the nontraditional worship service that we enjoyed.

Here are some best practices for keeping alignment between your new worship community and the rest of the church:

- The people who lead the various worship communities should meet for fellowship and team time regularly. Where the leaders are aligned as one team—caring for one another, working together, and affirming their mutual commitment to the church's advancement—their trust and teaming spill over into the rest of the church.

- When there is disagreement among these leaders, there must be clarity in terms of how the disagreement is to be resolved. In most cases, a team captain (or lead pastor) will make the final call. Everyone else must agree that they will fully honor the team captain's decisions. Occasionally, we will see teams of two or three pastors who attempt to work together in consensus. I have served on such a pastoral team, and it went well for us. The consensus style worked for us because of the high degree of trust and the time we spent together as a team. However, there should still be one pastor who is designated with clear authority to break a tie or a logjam in consensus.

- In all cases, when pastors or senior leaders emerge from a team meeting, they should present a united front to the rest of the staff and to the church. When a pastor or worship community leader is unable to make peace around certain decisions or policies, it may be time for that leader to begin exploring new ministry opportunities beyond their current congregation.

- When the new worship community remains affiliated with and has branched off from an existing church, the new community should be following the same sermon series as the rest of the church, in most cases. This can be done through live preaching based on a common outline developed by the team or via a video feed, with one preacher preparing each week's message for all worship communities.[5]

- At Embrace Church in Sioux Falls, South Dakota, one of the worship community pastors (who preaches only four times a year) serves as the chairperson of the sermon series development process all year long.[6] In this way, there is a teaming between preaching pastors that is balanced and leans into the varied gifts around the table. This kind of deep teaming lends to long tenures for team members because everyone feels deeply valued.

- Practice church-wide emphases and initiatives as a rule. It is better for the whole church to have a mission Sunday or a stewardship-commitment Sunday than for these kinds of emphases to vary by worship service. Slight variations in the execution of church-wide emphases may be in order, as a matter of contextualization, but keep things as similar as possible.

- Where worship communities meet in different locations, there are visible ways in which the different locations can signal alignment, such as having a similar look to the coffee area, having similar color schemes or décor in the lobby, and posting identical signage leading into the children's area.

- There should be one vision team for the church that oversees ministry in all locations and in all worship gatherings. Any teams that exist for the execution of ministry for a particular campus or worship community must understand the boundaries within which they can make decisions and/or contextualize the ministry.

Many long-tenured staff members will be unable or unwilling to adjust their leader practices to resource an increasingly complex church in multiple worship communities. Some staff may need to leave a church whose organizational structure is outgrowing their personal leader skills and preferences. This should not be a matter of shame; in most cases, it is simply a matter of preference in ministry styles. When a ministry grows beyond our comfort level (usually meaning toward a focus on more administration and less direct people contact on the ministry's front lines), we should look for a church with a simpler organizational structure. Some leaders function best in a church with an attendance somewhere between 400 and 800. When the church gets larger and more complicated, their stress level increases and their fun decreases. In these cases, it is probably time to move to a new job at a new church.

If they choose to stay and they do not have the skills to oversee a larger-scale ministry, they should be prepared to accept a demotion in the organization and to lose their direct-report relationship with the lead pastor.

Keeping a church aligned as it grows takes work. Because such alignment affects staff, it can be messy. But woe unto the church that decides alignment is not worth the trouble. That church will experience one or

both of the following: They will be "mysteriously" unable to grow, and/
or they will move into a season of passive-aggressive behavior and below-
the-surface conflict that sabotages their ministry.

29

LAUNCHING WITHIN AN AFRICAN AMERICAN CONTEXT

Candace Lewis

If you are answering the call to create and launch a new, contextual worship experience reaching African Americans or persons of African descent, thank you! As you embark upon this exciting ministry journey, I would invite you to consider at least four things: Consider your **call,** the **community** in which you're launching this new service, the current church **context,** and who will **collaborate** with you in this new adventure.

God continues to call on us to launch new worship experiences to connect people. God's call to launch something new may initially seem to the person receiving it as if it came out of nowhere. Yet as that same person looks back over their life experiences, they remember that they are a self-starter. They see challenges and injustices and wonders what can be done to address them. They are not content sitting on the sidelines, complaining that no one attends church any longer. They are action-oriented, always wrestling with solutions to the challenges facing both the larger society and their local community.

Maybe you are such a character, discerning such a call! It's time to say "yes" and get started.

As you answer your call, consider the community to which you are called. Are there existing Black churches in this community? If so, start by thinking like a community organizer and visit each church. Ask questions of the current pastor and leaders to understand who they are, what they offer, and what's missing. Keep good notes on what you learn. Remember that the new service you are called to launch can help to fill in the gaps you discover. Then, beyond interviewing the pastors, talk to several community residents, as diverse a group as possible from one community to the next. Let *them* teach you what is missing and needed.

I speak as one who has planted and who currently coaches African American church planters. I have done research and been a part of research studies on African American church planting. I want to assure you, there is still a critical need for African Americans to launch what you are called to launch! Just make sure that what you want to offer doesn't already exist in your community. As you begin to think through the type of service you are going to launch, let's think about how the Black Church has evolved. This historical perspective will help you build a bridge from the past to the present, reaching into the future.

First, let's understand that some mainline denominations started Black churches after slavery ended, and some leaders left The Methodist Church because they weren't allowed to pray. Richard Allen was one such leader, and he started a new denomination called the African Methodist Episcopal Church. The Negro Church, then the Black Church, grew through Reconstruction, well into the Civil Rights era. In the 1980s, Black communities saw the rise of nondenominational, Word, charismatic and evangelical, prosperity gospel-centered large churches. Some large churches adopted a "megachurch" mindset, which seemed to focus primarily on an individual, self-focused faith journey. Unfortunately, in many cases, they failed to hold the individual challenge of self-actualization in tension with the historic Black Church commitments to both individual faith formation and collective community transformation.

This departure of focus from that of historic Black churches has resulted in a consumerist situation where people drive into a neighborhood for worship and leave the neighborhood without any social transformation. There are exceptions, but far too many churches have a minimal impact upon the people in the surrounding community.

I believe we are now moving into a different era. This new season invites a new type of planter-leader to start new, relevant worship experiences for African Americans who will worship, serve, and have an impact upon the communities in which they reside. Remember, many Black churches today are beset with aging leadership, no succession plan, expensive facilities, empty seats, and mounting debt, as Black young adults opt to watch a worship service online and then head to Sunday brunch. These and other realities remind us of the need to start new, contextual, community-focused worship experiences in an African American context.

Assured of your call and your understanding about the community that you will serve, let's consider your context and your collaborators. First, your context. Let me start by sharing the story of a church planter. Claudia is in her early forties and has answered the call to start a new worship expression in her city. Most of the churches in her city are not effectively connecting with the young families. Neither are they able to garner the attention of the people who are "done with the church," nor the residents of the gentrified neighborhoods. Through conversations, interviews, and surveys, Claudia discerned a call to start a new worshiping community that can also be a Fresh Expression of church.[1] She has connected with leaders in her denomination who support her vision. She imagines a space that will include worship, yoga, a coffee bar, and a coworking space. She imagines a venue for transformational conversations. Claudia is not solely focused on gathering a critical mass of people to "launch" a new worship service. Yet worship remains a key part of her vision. She is envisioning how this new service can help impact the community and create a new ministry context that responds to the interest and needs of the community.

So, let's say that, like Claudia, you have established your particular context. Now, let's consider who will do this with you: Who can you collaborate with in the launch of this new worship experience? Claudia has found a partner in another new church in her city, a church with a very fresh approach to ministry and a multiethnic congregation. She has served on their team. Claudia is building a new launch team and developing leaders who will help launch every aspect of the next ministry start-up adventure. This team consists of people who want to share in the responsibilities for worship, community transformation, social justice, discipleship, mission, and administration.

Are there existing churches in the community that could partner with you in this new launch? Are you developing a core team of like-minded people who want to see this new ministry come to life in this community? Too many planters try to carry too much on their own shoulders and fail to develop a strong team in their first year. I am reminded of the scripture in Ecclesiastes 4:9-12:

> Two are better than one, because they have a good reward for their toil. For if they fall, one will lift up the other; but woe to one who is alone and falls and does not have another to help. Again, if two lie together, they keep warm; but how can one keep warm alone? And though one might prevail against another, two will withstand one. A threefold cord is not quickly broken.

You are called to a people and a place with a vision to launch something very contextual to the community in which you lead and serve. As your vision for this new something becomes clearer, what will you do to cultivate resources to get started? Many people who are called to start a new service already have a day job, so they don't have to add to their concerns the pressure of ensuring that the new worship service becomes financially sustainable on a specific timeline (all the more reason for focusing on team development early on). And when a new ministry leader makes her living from a source beyond the church, money collected in the early months can be reinvested in growing the new worship service and having a positive effect upon the community.

You will want to ask yourself, what are some of the problems or challenges people in this community face that people connected to this new service can address? As we navigate the 2020s, the new worship service you are considering might kick off as a digital experience and move toward a hybrid of on-site and online activities. Whatever you're envisioning, just remember to stay focused on connecting with the community. Pay attention to your context: It is distinct from anybody else's. And collaborate with the people God has placed in that community to join forces with you in creating a ministry for transformation.

30

PRACTICING
MULTIPLICATION
FROM THE START

Paul Nixon

About ten years ago, I sat down with a retired bishop in the Philippines, who explained to me how, in the late twentieth century, a somewhat socially isolated middle-class denomination in his country began growing again, quite rapidly.[1] They did so by creating a structural mechanism that strongly encouraged every Methodist church in the country to adopt a place of ministry beyond its local church building. As the relationships with their neighbors matured in their varied chosen mission outposts, Bible study groups would begin; and, eventually, new worship services would launch. But before any worship service would launch in a ministry outpost, the people in that emerging faith community would choose *yet another place* that would become *their* ministry outpost. They would choose their ministry outpost before they held their first worship service, thus ensuring that they were always working two ministry territories.

Always Thinking About the Next Place: The Baseball Diamond Analogy

When I returned to the United States, my Filipino American colleague Bener Agtarap (the author of chapter 7 in this book) worked with me to create an easy-to-understand analogy for how this unfolds. We chose a baseball diamond as the analogy.

Home Plate: Think of the existing congregation as standing on home plate, up to bat. As they seek to be faithful and effective baseball players, this church's leaders and members hit the ball and begin running the bases, from home to first to second to third, and so on.

First Base: When they get to first base, the church has chosen a new place, at least one mile from their current worship location, to begin a regular ministry presence of serving their neighbors. It might be any sort of ministry, in response to demonstrable human need and within the imagination and skill set of the church. Over the months, the ministry develops quite a host of people in the new neighborhood who have begun to trust the church people and to work alongside them in serving. In many cases, the pioneering ministry has to do with the neighborhood children. In other cases, the ministry is related to the poorest persons, who live with food insecurity and/or housing insecurity. In current American United Methodist lingo, think of any kind of Fresh Expression or other ministry that gathers people and begins to cultivate aspects of the kingdom of God in the neighborhood.

Second Base: Eventually, a subset of the adults (who are being served or who are helping to serve) is ready for something more. Organic community emerges as people hang out after the official ministry times to enjoy one another's company. And intentional faith exploration or faith-formation ministry often begins. This could be a ministry of small groups or a Bible class, something where people sit down and begin to reflect together upon life in the light of Christian faith. More months pass, and a few of the people may decide to become Christian, and still others resolve to reactivate their faith. A readiness for worship approaches in the neighborhood.

Third Base: A new worship community is launched in the neighborhood, drawing upon all the relationships made at the first and second bases as potential launch team members for the new service. But before the worship begins, the launch team makes *two* big choices: (1) when and where to hold weekly worship in their neighborhood; and (2) what nearby neighborhood will they adopt as their mission service zone. With the second choice, they begin (from second base) to run an entirely new baseball diamond, where they will go to a new first base (starting up a ministry of service), and so on. They start their new worship *and* the new service ministry at another location—simultaneously.

Back to Home: The new worship community has now matured and grown. It has the necessary leaders and has reached the necessary critical mass to basically take care of itself and cover its own costs in full. It thanks the mother church, which invested countless Sunday afternoons helping to plant it. At this point, the mother church celebrates this victory and chooses *yet another place* to begin serving neighbors, starting another run around the bases. Meanwhile, the new church is now well on its way to developing its own ministry to the people at its chosen mission location.

You get the idea! Multiplication of ministry is not something to think about next year or after crossing a certain threshold in the growth of the new worship community. Multiplication becomes a part of life from day one with any new ministry. Choosing *a next place* is a great way to reorient any church from a maintenance mode to a ministry-multiplication mode.

Always Thinking About the Next Leaders: The Railroad Track Analogy

Recently, I attended Embrace Church in Sioux Falls, South Dakota, and spent the better part of a Sunday morning studying what happened at the coffee bar in the lobby of their 57th Street Campus. At the 8:00 a.m. service, one particular guy makes the coffee. He loves to get up early, and this is his ministry. I watched him closely that morning as he made the first pots, but at some point I lost sight of him. He wasn't at the coffee bar anymore. Then I saw two other people working the coffee bar and talking to people as they arrived for the early service. Over the course of the morning, it became clear to me that coffee-making was a tag-team affair. The guy who makes the coffee was teaching me something important: Every great ministry team is constantly making space for someone else to step up and serve.

If I had stopped paying attention to the coffee bar, I might have assumed that it was a one-man show. This is how much of ministry works: One dedicated servant shows up week-after-week, year-after-year, until he or she moves away or dies, and then we begin looking for a replacement who will basically give up every Sunday of his or her life for the next twenty years to do what the last servant did. I get tired just thinking about it, and if I approach you to ask you to volunteer for this, one of two things will happen: (1) If you have decent boundaries and common sense, you will run away from me as fast as you can move! (2) If I catch you at a weak moment or you have a need to be needed, I pass to you a job that will busy you for a long time, even as your spouse glares at me.

The Embrace Church coffee ministry is a constantly morphing team, onboarding new people and inviting seasoned coffee servants to step aside from their accustomed shift to make space for others. There are probably a dozen people on the team who collectively work that single coffee station. And there are several additional coffee stations. When it is time to open a new campus, three or four of these coffee servants—and maybe a couple other coffee-making alums—will form a new team at the new place, easy as pie.

The reason Embrace learned how to do this was because they grew really fast in their early years (about 40 percent each year). I was their coach in those early days. When we saw the rate of growth, we would look at one of their ministries, such as Embrace Kids, and we would ask: At the rate we are growing, how much more space and how many more leaders will we need *by this time next year* to keep up? Or I could frame it in terms of a train racing across the Great Plains: This train is running at a high speed, and, based upon that speed (which at the time was 40 percent annual growth), we need to figure out how much additional railroad track we need to build in front of the train to prevent a derailment!

All year, every team leader would be faced with the challenge, how do I grow this team by this much, and how do I create this much more space? The church would sometimes add an additional ministry hour at one location or start a ministry hour at another place to add "railroad track," and they would seek to grow the fellowship of leader-servants in every ministry to ensure that the ministry infrastructure was ready for the train to barrel on through without disaster.

In ministries more complex than coffee-making, serious mentoring is required if a team is going to replicate itself. New leaders must be nurtured and allowed to shine. When a team still has the same high-profile ministry-leader star year after year, that is the mark of a church organized against ministry multiplication. So, people who mentor others and (temporarily) work themselves out of a job should be applauded! A great book that unpacks the art of mentoring in a church setting is *Hero Maker: Five Essential Practices for Leaders to Multiply Leaders,* by Dave Ferguson and Warren Bird. I have used this book with scores of church leaders who are trying to shift into multiplication mode.

Before you get any farther into this new worship community project, I invite you to pull together several of the people who are committed to it and ask them:

- How are we going to be a church that runs the baseball diamond(s)?
- And how will we organize ourselves to build enough new miles of railroad track so that we can get to the place God wants us to be by this time next year, without derailment?

Ultimately, multiplication is a leader development challenge. It requires thinking ahead to how many leaders we will need by the time we get to certain mileposts. And it requires an understanding of leadership that is more about empowering others than trying to do all the work ourselves.

31

DEVELOPING FINANCIAL SUSTAINABILITY

Gary Shockley

The ultimate goal in starting a new worship community isn't simply to get it off the ground. It's all about getting it *into orbit* so that it can stay around as a blessing to your city or region for years to come. If NASA only cared about putting enough fuel into a rocket to launch it into the air without exceeding the bounds of gravity, there would be a very loud thud, followed by a thoroughly destructive explosion as it comes crashing back to earth. Your aim isn't simply to get your new thing off the ground, but to develop enough systems so that it is viable and sustainable for the long haul.

For a new worship community to reach and sustain orbit, you and the leaders around you must share God's dream for the new thing and invite people to exercise generosity to support it.

And the leaders have to get there first. You simply cannot ask anyone else to do what you, yourself, haven't done. As a leader, think of yourself as the thermostat of your organization or faith community. Your values and behaviors will either increase or decrease the stewardship temperature around you. Please take a moment to read 1 Chronicles 29. These last pages of this book will await you after you read.

Note the domino effect of support for the building of God's Temple, starting with David (the king and chief leader), to the leaders of the tribes of Israel, and then the generals and captains of the army, and on to the king's administrative officers. Note how, when the people observed the generosity of all these leaders, they rejoiced and gave freely and whole-heartedly to the Lord; "and King David was filled with joy" (v. 9, NLT). Leaders always, always, always go first! And as they go first, they provide direction and opportunity for everyone else to find their way. Here are eleven ways effective leaders do this:

1. **Effective leaders cast a clear and compelling vision that answers the question, "Why do we exist?" And they repeat this vision, often and in as many ways as possible.** Remember, if you can't see it, neither will anyone else. Preach it, write it, teach it, live it! The leader does not necessarily have to be the one who discerns the vision; vision can emerge in a multitude of ways. But she must be the one who holds the community accountable to it, constantly celebrating it and reminding them of it joyfully.

2. **Effective leaders invite people to give willingly and joyfully to support God's work** (as shared in the vision) and *not* to support the budget or maintenance of the church. Do you believe that this ministry is an extraordinary investment opportunity? Do you deeply believe in where God is taking your church? If not (on either count), you have a problem.

3. **Effective leaders provide tools that will help people take better care of their household finances.** Allowing members to learn from an ethical financial planning resource can help people reduce their debt, budget their finances, and maximize their generosity to do God's work. People under the age of forty-five are facing financial pressures from slow career starts, tough job markets, rising healthcare costs, and high student-loan debt. It is a very different environment from what their parents faced only a generation ago.

These people would love to live out their faith and generosity in supporting God's work in the world, but for many of them, serious personal financial planning will be required for them to be able to do so.

4. **Effective leaders make stewardship a yearlong emphasis rather than a seasonal event.** When planning weekly sermons and worship events, be intentional about how the value of good stewardship will be expressed. People expect stewardship to be only a fall-season thing; surprise them! If you survey the most vital churches in America that are reaching people under the age of forty-five, you will notice that the annual pledge campaign no longer exists in many places. Yet these churches promote a high commitment and a more "all-in" discipleship vision than many older congregations.

5. **Effective leaders think about people's needs, not the church's needs.** This goes back to your personal theology about giving. If you believe giving is good for the giver and is in line with God's will for us, then you can speak into the benefits of giving as a response to God and not just to the needs of the church. Stewardship is a faith lifestyle, first and foremost; that is why Jesus talked about it so much. Never in the Gospels does Jesus connect the relationship of believers and money with church fundraising—not once!

6. **Effective leaders accentuate the positives by sharing stories of life transformation.** As an old proverb says, "Tell me the facts, and I'll learn. Tell me the truth, and I'll believe. But tell me a story, and it will live in my heart forever." Regular testimonials in the worship service (whether live or by video) are gold. You can share them on your website if you record them. Reminding your people of the difference that their church is making life-by-life is a clear signal to them that their church is worth their investment. (Remember, just because people catch on to the joy of giving does

not mean that they have decided that your particular church is a wise investment.)

7. **Effective leaders cultivate relationships with major donors.** Most churches seem to be blessed with a few folks who have both a greater abundance of financial blessings *and* the spiritual gift of giving. Learn who they are and help them to exercise their gifts. This honors them and invites them into greater joy. It may be helpful for the pastor or someone on the core leaders team to sit down annually with families who give above a certain amount, simply to get their feedback about the ministry and to thank them for their ongoing support. Major donors do not have to be members of your church, but they do have an interest in the community's thriving. Your ministry is, in part, the answer to something that they deeply long for.

8. **Effective leaders provide as many options as they can to help people give. Consider online giving, giving kiosks, and gift-texting as alternatives to passing the collection plate.** Ultimately, you want your community members to set up some kind of regular, automated giving online—contribution methods that become a dependable base of income month to month.

9. **Effective leaders are transparent in their reporting about finances.** People give when they have confidence that their leaders are handling finances well. Don't post your church's giving stats in your bulletin (this has been proven to be demotivating, especially to newcomers), but instead, provide a link people can follow to find an up-to-date report on the church's finances. Often in young communities, there are financial challenges. Addressing these issues without anxiety is important when leaders gather. Most people have enough financial worries of their own without adopting the church as another thing to worry about.

10. **Effective leaders thank people often and in a variety of ways.**
Regular statements of giving sent to people's homes is helpful; but,
as a leader, consider *hand-writing* short notes of gratitude to your
givers. Some people have discovered great benefit in writing a note
to someone who has given to the church for the very first time.
This unexpected acknowledgment goes a long way in cultivating
generosity. For those with challenged penmanship, slow it down,
and write slowly; the personal touch of a handwritten note is powerful. When our penmanship is lacking, a certain vulnerability is
added to our leader persona. Trust God, and mail the note!

11. **Effective leaders are realistic.** They are prepared to modify
their expectations of how a worship community might be able to
support a full-time pastor or pay for expensive real estate. Create
a business plan that includes a strong stewardship development
component as the leading funding stream but not the *only* funding stream!

Finally, when you are promoting generosity in your church, resist a
"one-size-fits-all" approach. Gain an understanding of the generational
distinctiveness that is present in your setting, and work at finding contex-
tually appropriate ways to communicate your vision and invite support.
Communicating to a ninety-year-old and a nineteen-year-old in the same
way doesn't make sense. Do the work required to make your message stick.

32

GO, REMEMBER, AND BE BLESSED!

Craig Gilbert

"Play Like a Champion Today"

Laurie Wenger was a native of South Bend, Indiana. She studied commercial art in high school and eventually got a job painting signs for the Athletic and Convocation Center at the University of Notre Dame. Though she was blind in one eye, she painted all kinds of signs while she was there. She even painted footballs, one of which sits in the Ronald Reagan Presidential Library to this day.

In November 1985, Laurie was asked to paint a special sign for the then-new football coach, Lou Holtz. Holtz had uncovered a photo of a sign in the locker room from an old book he had found. The sign was gone. No one remembered who had taken the sign down. No one really remembered the sign ever being there at all. In fact, no one is even sure what book Holtz was looking at when he saw the picture. But Coach Holtz wanted the sign for his locker room. Laurie was given the assignment. She sawed a piece of plywood; carefully primed and painted it with a gold background; and then, in blue, she hand-painted in her own personal style the words she had been given by the coach: *Play Like a Champion Today.*

Lou Holtz's intention was to remind his players each and every time they left the locker room that they represented a legacy of champions, and their play should reflect that heritage. Each player was asked to touch that sign as he ran out of the locker room, cementing that memory. Almost overnight, the sign became a tradition, and the tradition became one more story in the legend that is Notre Dame football.

And Laurie Wenger? Well, she went on to personally hand-paint more than 600 of those signs. Her personal hand-formed lettering even became a font of its own, trademarked as "Laurie." She is now enshrined as a beloved part of Notre Dame lore. Her work stands as a reminder to all Notre Dame fans and alumni that to be from Notre Dame is to be associated with champions.[1]

One of the most common elements shared in any worship service—no matter the style, denomination, and so on—occurs at the end. In more traditional settings, worship ends with a benediction; in more-modern settings, it may just be some sort of announcement. But I believe that at its best, the end of any worship service should be a reminder of who we are, what we do, and who we follow. This reminder mirrors the way the story of Jesus ends in the Gospel of Matthew. It is there that Jesus gives what we call the Great Commission. It is a command to go, to make disciples, to baptize, and to teach. But most significant is the accompanying promise in the final phrase, "And surely I am with you always, to the very end of the age" (28:20, NIV). What Jesus is saying to his disciples here is, no matter what . . . remember me, always, and be blessed.

A benediction is both a blessing and a reminder of whose we are. It is one last word to the people of God that there is more to being a follower of Christ than going to church. We are who we are, and we do what we do because of *whose we are*. While the intention of the locker-room sign at Notre Dame was to remind the football team players that they represent the history of their school in order to inspire greatness, a Christian bene-diction is even bigger. It is one last reminder that Christ is sending us out into the world, connected to *the why*. So now, just as we would end a worship service, I want to end this book with a benediction.

Therefore go and make disciples of all nations

From these words, remember two things. First, never lose sight of the fact that you must go out before you can expect anyone to come in. The days of just opening the doors of the church and expecting that people will come inside are long past. As Jesus taught in the parable of the great banquet, God sends God's servants out to find and invite people to come to God's feast (see Luke 14:15-24). You and your friends must first go out and invite others to come and meet God in worship.

Second, remember that you are building a service for new people. This is so the mission and ministry of your church can better reflect the call to make disciples *of all nations*. It will be easy to return to all the old habits and ways of worship that feel familiar. Place the faces of new people in front of you to remind you that you are going out to invite a whole new set of people to worship God with you.

Baptizing them in the name of the Father
and of the Son and of the Holy Spirit

It is not enough to bring new people in and think that you have succeeded in achieving your call. As you worship with them, just as you invited them to the party, you should also invite them to become believers. Go for it! Don't stop short of inviting them to the very best you have to offer. Worship alongside them. Share with them what God has done for you. Hear deeply their stories and their hearts, so that you can share the good news in a way that cuts past the cartoon Christianity that may have kept them at a distance. Help them find and embrace God for themselves and become followers of Christ.

And teaching them to obey everything
I have commanded you

There are many chapters of this book dedicated to making disciples by building community through prayer, hospitality, children's ministry, and more. The journey doesn't end at baptism. It doesn't end with another member identifying with Christ or with your church. It continues until all are truly living the good news of Jesus in their lives.

And surely I am with you always,
to the very end of the age

Here is the best part: You are not doing this on your own. When you go out to find new people, Jesus goes before you, preparing the way. When you meet and talk to new people, Jesus is with you, in and around each word you speak and around the words they speak. When they come to your new worship gathering, Jesus is waiting to welcome them. When you worship God together with them, Jesus is there, receiving and blessing their praises. When they are baptized, Jesus is standing as witness to their faith. When you join with them to study and learn from scripture, Jesus is there, opening hearts and minds to receive what God is providing to all. And when it is all said and done, when you have finished this journey and continue on to the next, Jesus is waiting to receive you and say, "Well done, good and faithful servant. Come and share in your God's happiness" (Matt. 25:23, AP).

I would love to tell you to relax, go, and have fun as you embark on this incredible adventure. Paul Nixon, my coauthor, finds a way to have fun with nearly everything he does. I do pray that this will be a fun, enjoyable experience; I really do! But fun is often fleeting—rarely permanent.

What lasts is the *joy* and satisfaction that comes from knowing that you are following God's call. It is the peace you hold in the promise that

Jesus is always with you. These are the things that will carry you through the successes—and the difficulties—that are to come.

There are going to be tough times as you do this. And in those moments, you won't be feeling the fun. Only your faithfulness to the call of God and your determined trust in the love Jesus has for you will hold you on course when everything seems to be going sideways.

Throughout this book, we have been sharing with you our insights, our experiences, our knowledge, our successes. But, make no mistake: Most of this knowledge has been gained through many failures as well. We have shared all of this trying to inspire; guide; and, yes, *excite* you as you create a new worship community.

So go, and remember who has called you to this work. Remember who goes before you. Remember why you follow. Remember what has been given to you so that you can give it to others. Remember where your faith lies. Remember that worship service in your past, where you decided to get real about your faith. Remember who stands with you when it seems everything and everyone else has left you. Remember to whom all glory is due when you succeed. Remember, when you reach the end of the journey and you understand that Christ has been in front of you, with you, and behind you all along. Remember . . .

And be blessed!

ABOUT THE AUTHORS AND CONTRIBUTORS

Paul Nixon is CEO of the Epicenter Group and director of Church Multiplication for Discipleship Ministries with The United Methodist Church. Epicenter exists to coach and equip transformational spiritual leaders for the twenty-first century. Epicenter's work is presently focused mostly within the United States and the United Kingdom. Paul is the author of ten previous books. He lives on both the east and west coasts of North America—in Washington, DC, and in Southern California— each of which is decidedly challenging for twenty-first-century church development.

Craig Gilbert is a worship consultant and founder of Purposed Heart Ministries. From Craig's ministry start in a small congregation to his serving a church with eight distinctive worship communities involving more than 2,000 worshipers, Craig has planned and presented worship in a wide variety of styles at the "every Sunday" level, as well as designing and leading worship in large conference settings for thousands of people. In every church Craig has served, he has helped to launch a new worship service. Each time, the services were well received from the start and grew quickly. Craig continues to consult every day with many congregations on how to strengthen their teams and systems to nourish great worship communities, including beginning new services.

Friends of Epicenter Group who have contributed chapters to this book include the following:

- **Bener Agtarap** is a pastor, a church planter, and a disciple-making movement multiplier. His ministry journey began as a church planter in the Philippines. He serves as Executive Director of Community Engagement & Church Planting/ Path 1 and as Director of Connectional Mobilization at Discipleship Ministries of The United Methodist Church. Bener is the coauthor with Curtis Brown of *Ready, Set, Plant: The Why and How of Starting New Churches* and co-editor with Doug Ruffle and Emily Reece of the training curriculum *Lay Planting in Today's World: Engaging All People with Jesus' Love.*
- **Beth Ann Estock** is an Integral Master Coach™ who helps leaders develop the capacities needed for ministry in the twenty-first century. Beth is the author of *Discernment* (2019) and the coauthor with Paul Nixon of *Weird Church* (2016). Beth lives in Portland, Oregon.
- **Derek Jacobs** is the founding pastor of The Village United Methodist Church in DeSoto, Texas, an African American-majority suburb of Dallas. The Village Church was preparing to move into their first facility and launch the ministry there when the worldwide COVID-19 pandemic hit, forcing them to "up their game" digitally!
- **Candace Lewis** is the president-dean of Gammon Theological Seminary in Atlanta, Georgia. Candace previously served as a church planter in Florida and as director for United Methodist church planting.
- **Dan Pezet** is district superintendent for the Charlotte Metro District of the Western North Carolina Annual Conference of The United Methodist Church. Before he attended seminary, Dan

served alongside Paul Nixon on the launch team of a new faith community in Florida.

- **Gary Shockley** is director of Equipping Vital Congregations of the Susquehanna Annual Conference of The United Methodist Church. Gary has served as a church planter, a large-church pastor, a national director for church planting, and a stewardship-development coach focused on capital fundraising.

- **Kay Kotan** is the founder of You Unlimited and Impressions Unlimited. Author and coauthor of more than a dozen books on church leadership and transformation, Kay has coached hundreds of churches and leaders across the United States. Her latest project is leading The Greatest Expedition, an initiative in church revitalization involving a large cast of expert practitioners and thought leaders. Kay lives in the Kansas City area.

- **Kim Griffith** is executive director of Griffith Coaching and Founder of Looking Glass. A former church planter, Kim specializes in coaching, team development, and workshops equipping leaders for success. Kim lives in central Florida.

- **Kim Shockley** is coordinator for Pathways of Spiritual Leadership of the Susquehanna Annual Conference of The United Methodist Church. She is the coauthor with Paul Nixon of *The Surprise Factor: Gospel Strategies for Changing the Game at Your Church*.

- **Kris Sledge** is the founding pastor of The Journey in Harrisburg, Pennsylvania, a multiethnic new church in a city with a history of persistent racial segregation.

- **Matt Temple** is associate director of New Starts for the North Texas Annual Conference of The United Methodist Church and co-pastor at Newstory Church in Chicago. Newstory is a fully affirming, multicultural, multiracial, multiethnic nondenominational church in Chicago.

- **Rachel Gilmore** is a church planter working in partnership with Central United Methodist Church in Phoenix, Arizona. Previously, she served as founding pastor of The Gathering in Virginia Beach and as Director of Recruiting, Assessing and Training for Church Planters at Discipleship Ministries.
- **Sandy Gutting** is administrative assistant for Congregational Development of the Alabama-West Florida Annual Conference of The United Methodist Church. Among Sandy's passions are great hospitality at church and her beautiful grandkids.
- **Tyler Sit** is the pastor and church planter of New City Church in Minneapolis, Minnesota. He is also author of *Staying Awake: The Gospel for Changemakers*, an exploration of Christianity that centers queer people of color.

NOTES

Orientation

1. Gulf Breeze Church in Northwest Florida grew from 1,000 to 2,200 in weekly worship attendance between 1993 and 2002, due in large part to the relaunch of one of its worship communities and the addition of three more worship communities within this time frame. During this remarkable season, 1,300 persons joined the church by profession of their faith in Christ.

2. Charles Arn, *How to Start a New Service: Your Church Can Reach New People* (Grand Rapids, MI: Baker Books, 1997).

3. I served as Director of Congregational Development for the Alabama-West Florida Annual Conference of The United Methodist Church, 2002–2007. The years of net growth for that judicatory were 2003–2007.

4. Online worship attendance is commonly measured in terms of online engagement of thirty minutes or longer.

5. This refers to the Path 1 Team at The United Methodist Church's Discipleship Ministries (www.path1.org) and The Epicenter Group (www.epicentergroup.org).

6. If a chapter title appears in **bold** font in the table of contents, we feel it is important reading for the entire launch team. There are twelve chapters in this book that we recommend everyone read.

Chapter 1

1. Elaine Heath, *God Unbound: Wisdom from Galatians for the Anxious Church* (Nashville, TN: Upper Room Books, 2016), 76.

Chapter 2

1. This situation was once the leading reason why existing churches started new worship gatherings. Today, it is somewhat rare.
2. For perhaps half the churches that decide to start a new worship service designed for their neighbors, this decision means that the church may still be open for ministry ten years from now, as opposed to closing within the decade.
3. Meaning that the food is farm-to-table fresh, and meals are fully prepared on-site. Dinner church usually will not work with big-box-store frozen lasagna or carryout pizza.
4. I coach a church in Birmingham, UK, called Jazz Church. Jazz music is core to its identity and is a driver for almost everyone who chooses to walk in and try our church out.

Chapter 3

1. For a summary of Spiral Dynamics theory as it relates to Christian ministry, see *Weird Church: Welcome to the Twenty-first Century* by Beth Ann Estock and Paul Nixon (Cleveland, OH: The Pilgrim Press, 2016). Note especially the prologue, pp. v-xvi.
2. For more information on these four areas, see *Multiply Your Impact: Making the Leap from Church Maintenance to Gospel Movement* by Paul Nixon and Christie Latona (Fun & Done Press, 2013).
3. Sometimes a young adult leader or team member who has stayed connected to church (even as most of his or her peers have left) will turn out to be extremely rigid and will cling to old customs, impairing a church's missional alignment. And sometimes an older team member will offer strong advocacy for innovation and the disruption of old paradigms. The point is this: Don't be fooled by age!

4. Margaret Brunson is CEO of Illumined Leadership Solutions and a Leadership Coach for the North Carolina Annual Conference of The United Methodist Church.

Chapter 4

1. Chapter 14, "Thinking Through the Teams You Will Need," will help you build this list.
2. John Wesley's three simple rules are (1) Do no harm, (2) Do good, and (3) Stay in love with God. For more on this, see *Three Simple Rules: A Wesleyan Way of Living* by Reuben P. Job (Nashville, TN: Abingdon Press, 2007).

Chapter 5

1. Lewis Carroll, *Alice's Adventures in Wonderland*, Project Gutenberg, https://www.gutenberg.org/files/11/11-h/11-h.htm.
2. Nextdoor is a popular app that helps people connect with their geographic neighbors.
3. MissionInsite is a demographics tool that helps American ministry leaders discover what Big Data can teach them about their neighbors. It is based on census data, credit reports, and national surveys. www.missioninsite.com.
4. Gloo is a market analysis tool used by secular businesses and churches alike. www.gloo.us.
5. To explore further, see Paul Nixon's most recent book, *Cultural Competency: Partnering with Your Neighbors in Your Ministry Expedition* (Knoxville, TN: Market Square Publishing, 2021).

Chapter 6

1. For more details on bridge events, see Kay Kotan, *Gear Up!: Nine Essential Processes for the Optimized Church* (Nashville, TN: Abingdon Press, 2017) and Bob Farr, Doug Anderson, and Kay Kotan, *Get Their Name: Grow Your Church by Building New Relationships* (Nashville, TN: Abingdon Press, 2013).

Chapter 7

1. Junius Dotson, *Soul Reset: Breakdown, Breakthrough, and the Journey to Wholeness* (Nashville, TN: Upper Room Books, 2019), 51.

Chapter 9

1. Nett or NETT stands for Nations Experiencing Transformation Together.

Chapter 10

1. "Expert Opinion," *The Journey*, http://thejourneyharrisburg.org/index.php/expert-opinion/

Chapter 11

1. Jenna Goudreau, "So Begins a Quiet Revolution of the 50 Percent," *Forbes*, January 30, 2012, https://www.forbes.com/sites/jennagoudreau/2012/01/30/quiet-revolution-of-the-50-percent-introverts-susan-cain/?sh=1f0fb25d93fb.
2. Crowdcast (https://www.crowdcast.io) is a platform that allows multiple people to be live on screen at the same time, but attendees are represented by avatars, so they can answer polls, chat, and ask questions without being visible on-screen. It also allows people to register in advance and helps you retain information on the attendees. One additional feature of the platform that is appealing to faith communities is that it will automatically livestream your webinar to multiple social media platforms at the same time. A similar platform is StreamYard (https://streamyard.com).

Chapter 12

1. J. D. Payne, *Pressure Points: Twelve Global Issues Shaping the Face of the Church* (Nashville, TN: Thomas Nelson Publishers, 2013), 164.

Chapter 13

1. Many types of plastic chairs are more than adequate for sixty to ninety minutes of seating, even with a rather upscale crowd.

2. Lisa Cannon Green, "New Churches Draw Those Who Previously Didn't Attend," *Lifeway Research*, December 8, 2015, https://lifewayresearch.com//2015/12/08/new-churches-draw-those-who-previously-didnt-attend/.

3. Keeping the custodian assigned to your group happy is a valid ministry priority in and of itself.

Chapter 14

1. This may be a really big team, one that could be broken into at least three smaller teams for many worship communities (a design team, an onstage team, and a tech/offstage team).

2. The "80-20 Rule" is a well-documented phenomenon that shows up in almost every major category of human interaction. It is not a firm, mathematical law but an observed characteristic that applies in most ministry endeavors, including giving and outreach.

Chapter 15

1. The Bible does not teach that "money is the root of all evil." The actual verse says, "The love of money is a root of all kinds of evil" (1 Tim. 6:10).

2. David Steindl-Rast and Sharon Lebell, *Music of Silence: A Sacred Journey through the Hours of the Day* (Berkeley, CA: Ulysses Press, 1998), 25–26.

Chapter 16

1. Even if the pastor does not use a pulpit or podium, it is nice to have one for when others may speak who would feel more comfortable with a surface on which to place their notes.

Chapter 18

1. William H. Frey, "The US will become 'minority white' in 2045, Census projects," *Brookings*, March 14, 2018, https://www.brookings.edu/blog/the-avenue/2018/03/14/the-us-will-become-minority-white-in-2045-census-projects/. Since this article, the 2020 census documented that white population net decline had actually set in about five years faster than Brookings anticipated. So 2045 would now be a conservative estimate.

2. The Intercultural Development Inventory is a leading assessment tool for intercultural competencies in individuals and in teams. Intercultural competency is defined by IDI as "the capability to shift cultural perspective and appropriately adapt behavior to cultural differences and commonalities." www.idiinventory.com.

3. New City Church has benefited greatly from reading *My Grandmother's Hands: Racialized Trauma and the Pathway to Mending Our Hearts and Bodies* by Resmaa Menakem (Las Vegas: Central Recovery Press, 2017) and numerous others.

Chapter 20

1. The term *video view* refers to how many times a computer tuned in to a recorded worship experience online in a given timeframe. It does not specify the number of people, or necessarily specify how many repeat views or the amount of time per view. *Engagements* are a more general term—referring to any kind of online interaction.

Chapter 22

1. *Square* is a condition in building where two objects sit at perfect right angles to each other. It is the perfect alignment of the two right angles that creates the basis of both the regularity and the strength for a building to stand on its own.

2. If you would like to look further at this concept, I recommend reading *Worship in the Shape of Scripture* by F. Russell Mitman (Cleveland, OH: The Pilgrim Press, 2009). He clearly outlines worship as a story or conversation based on a variety of scriptural examples.

Chapter 26

1. "What Millennials Want When They Visit Church," Barna, March 4, 2015, https://www.barna.com/research/what-millennials-want-when-they-visit-church/.

Chapter 27

1. Charles Denman Awards are given for excellence in evangelism.
2. Joy Thornburg Melton, *Safe Sanctuaries: Reducing the Risk of Abuse in the Church for Children and Youth* (Nashville, TN: Discipleship Resources, 2008).

Chapter 28

1. By "common vision," we mean that all leaders rally around certain common features of the vision, not that each leader sees everything exactly the same. There are simply common denominators. For example, if I am to serve as a leader within a church, I need to be able to endorse the common denominators of that church's vision. If I have serious issues with parts of the common vision, then I need to look for another ministry team.
2. *Agreement* does not mean that everyone must be equally enthusiastic about every practice, but there is a respect for the understanding that "under this organizational umbrella, this is how we do things." An example of this might be the requirement that certain persons be present anytime a sacrament is celebrated. There may be room for debate as to whether these persons' presence is truly necessary in the eyes of God, but for purposes of organizational alignment, there is an agreed-upon protocol.
3. Paul Nixon, *Multi: The Chemistry of Church Diversity* (Cleveland, OH: The Pilgrim Press, 2019), 78.
4. This is a good rule for preaching/teaching pastors in general. In vital churches with very distinctive DNA that sets them apart from other congregations, great care must be given to interviewing potential leaders with a focus first on the church's distinctive vision.
5. Where there is extremely high trust between pastors, some churches may allow different worship themes between services and seek to build strong alignment in other ways. Given the horror stories that abound around poor alignment, extreme caution is in order when churches decide to diversify themes and preaching topics from one service to the next.

6. This pastor is Travis Waldrop, who is campus pastor for the Tea, South Dakota, Campus of Embrace Church. Adam Weber is the lead pastor at Embrace and preaches most Sundays of the year. Embrace has one preacher for all services each week, using video for most venues.

Chapter 29

1. For more information on Fresh Expressions, visit www.freshexpressions us.org.

Chapter 30

1. It was the same bishop—Bishop Emerito Nacpil (retired by 2011 when I interviewed him)—to whom Bener Agtarap referred in chapter 7.

Chapter 32

1. Paraphrased from the story "Laurie Wenger: 'Play Like a Champion Today'—A Simple Phrase Became Big Business" by John Walters, University of Notre Dame Strong of Heart: Profiles of Notre Dame Athletics, 2010, https://strongofheart.nd.edu/profiles/laurie-wenger-2010.